STUDENT-FRIENDLY GUIDES

Write great essays!

Write great essays!

A guide to reading and essay writing
for undergraduates and taught postgraduates

PETER LEVIN

Open University Press

Open University Press
McGraw-Hill Education
McGraw-Hill House
Shoppenhangers Road
Maidenhead
Berkshire
England
SL6 2QL

email: enquiries@openup.co.uk
world wide web: www.openup.co.uk

and Two Penn Plaza, New York, NY 10121-2289, USA

First published 2004, reprinted 2004, 2005

A catalogue record of this book is available from the British Library

ISBN 0 335 21577 7

Library of Congress Cataloging-in-Publication Data
CIP data applied for

Typeset by YHT Ltd, London
Printed in the UK by Bell & Bain Ltd, Glasgow

Contents

Part Five: Referencing styles

Part Six: Plagiarism and collusion

List of Tables

List of Boxes

The strange world of the university.
READ THIS FIRST!

The world of the university – the 'academic world' – is a world of its own. It's very different from the 'real world' in which you and I and most other people exist. If you're a student, it's crucial to your success that you are aware of the many differences between the two worlds and can move easily between them.

'Out there, in the real world, things happen and things change.' In the real world, people live and work, raise children, play or watch sport, go clubbing, and so on. There are lots of other human activities and processes going on as well, like manufacturing and trading and communicating and providing services of many kinds. Out there too are a host of natural phenomena: to do with the weather, all kinds of matter and energy, chemical reactions, the birth, growth and death of living things – you name it!

The academic world, on the other hand, is full of 'mental constructs': descriptions, theories and explanations, ideas and critiques. You and I can't experience such mental constructs in the same way that we experience the real world, directly, through seeing, hearing, touching, tasting, smelling. Instead we have to get them into our heads through the medium of – in particular – the written word and the spoken word, via books and articles and web pages, and the lectures that academics give. 'It is a peculiarity of academic learning that its focus is not the [real] world itself but others' views of that world.'[1]

What this means is that in the academic world you'll be learning at second hand, so to speak, rather than through your own experience, as you do in the real world. Learning at second hand does not come naturally to most people. You need some help. Sadly, such help is in short supply in the academic world. This series of guides is designed to fill that gap.

But differences in ways of learning are far from being the only differences between the academic world and the real world. You think you can read, right? In the academic world, you're probably wrong, on two counts.

First, if you're at university in an English-speaking country you may have the impression that the books and articles you're told or recommended to read are in English. Certainly the words and grammar look like English, but don't be misled: they're actually written in 'academic-speak'. Academic-speak is a long way removed from day-to-day spoken and written English. In particular, it makes far more use of abstract words and expressions: they exist in thought or as ideas but don't have a physical or concrete existence. So reading academic-speak is not the same as reading ordinary English. You've got to translate as you read, so it's much more like reading a foreign language, with lots of looking up words in the dictionary and puzzling over the grammar. Inevitably, it's a slow process at first. It takes time to become fluent.

What makes matters worse is that every subject has its own particular academic-speak. So if you're taking courses in several subjects, you have several 'foreign languages' to get used to. Don't let this discourage you: most people manage it! The secret is to be aware of what's going on: it makes those times when you feel you're not making progress much easier to cope with.

Second, you may arrive at university taking it for granted that 'reading' means something like 'starting a book at page 1 and reading all the way through to the end'. Beware! 'Reading' in the academic world means using books to find what you want in them. If you try to read everything on your so-called 'reading lists' all the way through you're heading for a nervous breakdown. Think of reading as a 'treasure hunt': an active search rather than an attempt to soak up and absorb everything you come across.

Other words too have strange meanings in the academic world. You think 'discuss' and 'argue' refer to conversations with other people? Forget it! In most essay-based subjects you'll have to discuss and produce arguments on your own.

In the academic world, students come and – after a time, when they've completed their courses – go. The academics (faculty, or teaching staff) mostly stick around for much longer. You may feel, having met a few, that academics are, by and large, a somewhat strange bunch. I have to say that that's my feeling too. They're certainly very individual – have you heard the joke that organizing academics is like herding cats? – many to the point of being idiosyncratic if not actually eccentric. Almost all of them are people who themselves did well as students at university and are now doing research as well as teaching. So the chances are that they're (a) quite talented at their subjects, and (b) quite preoccupied with their research work, especially as almost all academics get promotion on the basis of their research publications, not their teaching achievements.[2]

This can create quite a few problems for students. The pressure on academics to produce publications and perform administrative duties limits the time and energy they can put in to teaching. Moreover, talented people, people who have an intuitive flair for their subject, can be really poor at explaining it, because when they were students themselves, they were able to tackle it by leaps and bounds: they didn't have to go slowly, step by step, as mere mortals do. Although many academics are dedicated to teaching, most of them have had little or no training in how to teach. And what training there is conspicuously omits what is arguably the most important skill of all for a teacher: that of empathizing and developing rapport, without which a teacher has no chance of being able to put himself or herself in the shoes (and head) of a student grappling with a task.

As a student, you may also find that academics distance themselves from you in all sorts of ways. Unless you're really fortunate, you'll be treated not as a junior member of a learning community but as if you belong to a separate species. You'll be a distraction from research, a burden ('workload'). You'll be treated as one of the masses, to whom education is to be 'delivered'. You'll be someone in an audience, listening or trying to take notes while the speaker engages in that one-way mode of communication beloved of academics, telling other people what's what. You may well find, like the majority of students, that the feedback you get on your work isn't satisfactory.[3] In all probability it'll be mostly criticism rather than appreciation, focusing on bad points and ignoring the good ones, while at the same time not helping you to see what to do if you're to get better marks for your next piece of work. And at exam time you may experience the relationship with your teachers as a kind of game, in which you have to work out for yourself what the rules are for winning: what the examiners' expectations are, what approach, style etc. will be rewarded and what will be penalized.

I suspect that all institutions are capable of messing up the lives of the people who work for and within them. I don't see universities as an exception to this rule. At some point different academics will be giving you different and conflicting advice about some aspect of your work. And there will be mixed messages to look out for. For example, you may be given group projects to work on to develop your 'teamwork skills', and at the same time be warned very strictly against collaborating with other students on writing tasks: this is regarded as 'collusion' and will be punished!

Does all this sound very gloomy? I can't pretend that I don't think that the culture of higher education in the UK is in serious need of reform: I do. But for you that's a side issue. If you're to succeed as a student the first thing you have to do is to appreciate the nature of the system you've signed up to, which is why I felt it important to be absolutely realistic about it in this foreword. It's only when you know the system, warts and all, that you can formulate your own strategy for dealing with it. Without such a strategy, you'll have no confidence in what you're doing. You'll be looking anxiously all over the place for clues as to what you should be doing and how. You'll be dragged this way and that, all over the place, trying to keep up. It's like running after a bus, trying to catch it but never quite managing it, tiring yourself out and getting your lungs full of exhaust fumes in the process: a thoroughly frustrating experience.

In this series of student-friendly guides, my overall aim is to help you to take control of your studies, to be confident in what you're doing, and ultimately to get what you want out of your university experience – which I hope will include both fun and having your mind stretched. To this end I have done my best to demystify and make sense of the academic world, to address the many issues which students raise, and to suggest practical courses of action. I've tried to write in plain English, and to help you to deal with academic-speak. Whether you've come to university from school or FE college, or you're a mature student or an international student, I hope these guides will help you to master and enjoy your studies, and to win the qualification you're after.

Peter Levin

Introduction

My aim in writing this guide is to help you to read and write effectively and efficiently, so that you can write essays that your teachers appreciate and give good marks for, and do so in a way that makes best use of your time and energy.

The culture of higher education in the Western world is very much a culture of the written word. Even in the age of the internet, books and articles in journals are the prime medium for recording and disseminating thoughts, arguments, research reports, etc. Authors commit their message to paper and become publicly identified with what they write. Academics are appointed and promoted largely on the basis of their publications, and counts are made of 'citations' (mentions of their publications in someone else's). As a student, if your first question on starting a new course is 'Is there a set textbook?' you are in good company: we all feel reassured if we can hold 'the bible' in our hands when faced with a new and challenging experience.

Reading and writing at university level are closely connected. Most obviously, when writing essays you will have to draw on materials to be found in books and articles (also known as 'papers' when published in 'learned journals'). But, if you are doing your job properly, the two activities will also be linked in your own mind. As you think about the subject, your thoughts will provide you with a structured approach to both your reading and your writing, at one and the same time. Consider what happens when you're reading and a question comes into your mind. You carry on reading but now you are keeping a lookout for the answer to that question, and you may now be picturing your essay as having a section devoted to that question. Collecting and organizing your thoughts is a central part of both reading and writing.

With this in mind, in the following pages I offer answers to some of the questions I'm frequently asked, such as these:

● I'm trying to write an essay, and I've got this huge reading list: do I have to read everything? And where do I start?

- What kind of notes should I take? Is it best to aim to condense the books and articles that I read?

- I like to begin at the beginning of a book or article and carry on to the end, so I don't miss anything. Isn't that what I'm supposed to do?

- I'm a very slow reader. How can I read more quickly? Should I take a speed-reading course?

- When I sit down to read, after a while my mind keeps wandering. I wonder if I'm really suited for academic study: is there any point in my carrying on?

- I'm told I have to read critically. What does that mean?

- Some of what I have to read is really hard to understand. Am I stupid?

- I have to write a 2000-word essay, I've got heaps of notes, and I've already used 1000 words on my introduction. What should I do?

- How should I structure my essays?

- We've been warned very strongly against plagiarizing, but I'm not clear what I'm supposed not to do. Can you help?

- I've just had an assessed essay back with the comment: 'You have serious problems with your bibliography.' This doesn't exactly help me to do better. What do I have to do to get my bibliography right?

Of course, different people have different abilities, different ways of learning, and different styles of working. I cannot know what *your* particular ones are. I do know from the feedback I get that most of my suggestions work for most people, but you won't necessarily be one of them. And you may already have your own methods that work reasonably well for you and that you don't want to abandon.

So do treat what's in this guide not as absolute wisdom but as 'worth a try': see what you can use that works for you. I'm offering you suggestions, not telling you this is how you *must* do it.

It's also the case that different teachers and departments in universities up and down the country have different expectations of students and make different demands of them. Again, I can't be an expert in all of these, and I don't pretend to be. So what I aim to do is to offer you ways of discovering for yourself – by asking questions, by experimenting, by reading between the lines – the expectations and demands that *your* teachers place on you and your fellow students. I aim to help you to become your own expert on how to write for *your* teachers.

Part One

Getting started

'I'm a slow reader'

Many students tell me they're slow readers. When I ask them how they read, what they actually do when they sit down with a book, it always turns out that they take it for granted that they know what 'reading a book' is. It's an activity that consists of beginning to read at page 1 and carrying on until you reach the end at page 250 or whatever, when you've finished. This concept of 'reading' may be psychologically reinforced in a number of ways. You may feel guilty if you skip pages, and if you read the last chapter before you've read all the preceding ones. You may not dare to skip any pages in case you miss something important. And you may feel that 'reading all the way through' is what your teachers – authority figures – expect of you. Not surprisingly, reading the whole book takes a lot of time. And if you find that you never finish the reading before the essay deadline or the class, it can really sap your confidence.

So let's deal with that at the outset. Let me offer you a 'reframe' of your task. Your task is to find in the book those 'bits and pieces' – information, reasoning, ideas, theories, explanations, conclusions – that you want, that will help you to address the topic. Think of books as 'treasure chests'. Somewhere inside are the particular jewels that you require. You need a quick way of finding them. In this guide I offer you three strategies for doing exactly that.

As for feeling guilty if you don't read every word on every page, bear in mind that the book wasn't written for *you*. Nor was it written with your class or essay topic in mind. You are under no duty, no obligation, to read it all the way through. And a book of 250 pages contains around 100,000 words: you need to extract from it probably a few hundred at most, less than 1 per cent. Again, your task is not to 'read' the book in the traditional way; your task is to find what is relevant to your needs and capture it.

Observe how your task is transformed. It's no longer to absorb masses of words, to soak them up like a sponge: rather it is to do detective work, tracking down what you need. Happily, this is a task that most people's brains enjoy, and are well suited to, whereas soaking up masses of words is not. (If you've ever fallen asleep in a library you'll know what I mean.)

So here's the principle underlying the three 'reading strategies' that I offer in this guide: be an *active* reader, *interrogate* books, chapters and articles, *use* them to find what is relevant to *your* needs. This is really, really important. Don't be a passive reader, hoping that you'll absorb something from a book if you simply spend enough time with it. It's a forlorn hope: you'll attain nothing more than great depths of boredom.

There are two other factors that might cause you to find reading academic books and articles a very slow, time-consuming activity. One is that you feel obliged to take copious notes, which of course slows down your reading. The trouble is that on a first reading you don't know what is relevant, and consequently you are liable to note or highlight much, much more than you will need.

The second factor that slows down reading is that many academic books and articles are, to all intents and purposes, written in a foreign language, 'academic-speak'. Especially in a subject that is new to you, you have to translate the words on the page from academic-speak into language that you can understand, language that is familiar to you. Again, focusing your efforts on what is relevant to your needs will help you to make this a manageable task.

To sum up: abandon your preconceived notions of 'reading'. You're in the business of using books to find what you want. Teach yourself to be a detective. You might even have some fun!

Three stages in academic learning

Looking at what students actually do at university, it seems to me that academic learning proceeds in three repeating stages: (a) selecting and copying; (b) translating; and (c) digesting. Before you can digest new material you have to translate it into language you can understand, and before you can do this you have to select that material from the deluge that lands on you, and copy it down.

Table 1: Three stages in academic learning

Stage	Activities
Selecting and copying	Making notes
Translating	Paraphrasing and annotating
Digesting	'Engaging' with the subject, thinking and reasoning in the subject's language

Selecting and copying

Academic learning starts from other people's writing and lecturing and from group discussions – in classes, seminars and tutorials. This has important consequences for you. When you're learning something new, you necessarily have to start by selecting and copying other people's work.

You may know this activity as 'making notes': I describe it as '*selecting* and *copying*' to bring out the fact that you have to select what notes to take. In a lecture you will usually not be able to write down everything the lecturer says: you will try to select what seem to you the most important points, and write those down. Faced with a book, you won't be able to copy out or photocopy the whole book, so you'll try to select relevant passages. But when you first encounter this material you probably won't be in a good position to judge relevance: a common feeling at this point is 'I'll get down as much as I can now, and try to make sense of it later'.

Translating

When you first take notes, the words are those of the lecturer or writer: they still 'belong' to that person. To some extent this is unavoidable, because the subject matter is complex, there are tricky concepts to master, and every subject has its own jargon. So what you read or hear is 'academic-speak', the technical language of the subject. It will seem to you like a foreign language, even if your native tongue is English, and indeed it is best to treat it as such.

What makes matters worse is that much academic writing is poor. Some of it is awful. You are all too likely to come across writers who aren't consistent in the words they use, and who don't offer a decent 'map' to guide the reader through their material. They may fail to make their basic assumptions explicit, and omit steps in their reasoning. You may even encounter some whose command of English grammar, punctuation and sentence structure is weak. And many writers get badly 'languaged up', producing a flood not so much of 'academic-speak' as of gobbledygook.

This creates two nuisances that you have to deal with. First, it sets you a bad example and leads you to imitate this style of writing: it's worth making a conscious effort to resist this. Second, when you're reading this stuff it's really hard work to uncover the writer's meaning and reasoning. To make head or tail of it you have to translate it into language that you can understand, that makes sense to you, even if your native language is English. Indeed, I suspect that all intellectual learning actually involves an 'internal translation' process.

Translating involves expressing the statement on the page in front of you in different words, so you produce an 'equivalent' statement that, all being well, makes sense to you. That is to say, it involves you in *paraphrasing* the original statement. Usually you'll also find yourself *annotating* it: adding clarification, comments, explanations and cross-references.

Digesting

'Digesting' is the next and final stage in academic learning. 'To digest' is a metaphor: it is difficult to convey its meaning other than in terms of more metaphors: to take in, to assimilate, to absorb. Digesting a subject or topic entails getting to grips with it; learning to see it and think about it as your teachers do; appreciating its subtleties, its complexity and the significance of its various features; and becoming fluent in its language, so its words resonate with you.

You'll know that you are well advanced with digesting a subject, and have thus got well beyond selecting/copying and translating, when you can think and reason in the subject's language. Just as when someone asks you a question in Spanish, say, and you can answer immediately in that language without having to translate the question into English, formulate your answer in English and then translate your answer into Spanish.

▼ ▼ ▼

When it comes to reading, what are the implications for you of viewing academic learning as this three-stage process: selecting/copying, translating, digesting? For selecting and copying, you need to have some criterion of relevance for selecting material that you're going to copy into your notes. For translating purposes, you need to compile a kind of mini-dictionary for yourself, that you can have by you when you read. And for the purpose of digesting, you need – I suggest – to question what you read and hear. I'll say more about all of these later on in this book.

Coping with monster reading lists

If you have been issued with 'monster' reading lists, you have my sympathy. Such lists can be hugely intimidating, especially when you first encounter them. But there are ways of getting to grips with them.

First of all, though, what makes a reading list long? There can be several explanations. Many teachers are well aware that the demand to borrow books from the library always exceeds the supply, and so they may well include two or more books that cover the same ground – especially if it's basic material – to maximize the likelihood that you and your fellow-students will find that material somewhere. Clearly you don't need to read *all* the books that cover that ground. So if the list includes a number of basic texts, one will usually be sufficient.

A list may also be long because the teacher who compiled it intended it to be a comprehensive list of references on the subject or topic, to be used by students as a source of materials for in-depth essays or preparing for exams, as well as for seminar preparation. In this case the list ought to be divided into 'essential reading' (for seminars) and 'further reading' (for more advanced work), but this isn't always done. If it *is* done, concentrate on the essential reading; if it *isn't* done, ask your teacher for advice.

Finally, a list may be long because teachers have added new items as they have been published, but not 'weeded out' old ones. Books or journal articles more than ten or twenty years old (it'll vary from subject to subject) and that aren't classics may well have been superseded by more recent publications. My advice is to start with the most recent ones. Not only will they be more up-to-date: they may include summaries and critiques of the earlier material and will have more comprehensive lists of references. If your reading list doesn't include the dates of publication of books, ask your teacher to supply them. Failing that, look them up in the library catalogue.

One more point: keep your eye on the assessment ball. You need reading lists not only so that you write essays and participate in seminars but also so that later on you can revise for unseen (traditional) exams and write assessed essays. To write an unassessed essay earlier in the year it is not necessary to have made yourself an expert on the topic. Read three or four items. Identify significant conclusions and problematic issues and questions and write about those. That will move your learning on, and give you a basis to build on later.

To sum up:

- Where there are several basic texts on a reading list, one – or at most two – will usually be sufficient for writing an essay.
- Concentrate on essential reading.
- Look for the most up-to-date items.
- Bear in mind that the time that you'll need to be most in command of your topic is when you are being assessed. Until then, concentrate on learning.

Part Two

Reading purposes and strategies

What are you reading for?

It is really important, before you start reading a book, chapter or article, that you are clear in your mind *why* you are reading it, what you are reading it *for*. If you are reading aimlessly, the chances are that you will soon find yourself just idly turning the pages, then gazing at them without making sense of the words while your mind is somewhere else entirely. So whenever you start reading something, pause and ask yourself: 'Why am I doing this? What do I want to get out of it? What is my task, what's the job I have to do?'

Note that 'because it's on my reading list' is not *by itself* a sufficient reason for starting to read something. (Nor, indeed, is 'my teacher told me to'.) You really do need to have a specific *purpose*. There has to be something that you want to get from your reading.

You can read for different purposes and in different ways. In Table 2

I list four reading strategies – 'exploratory', 'dedicated', 'targeted' and 'can't stop, won't stop' – together with, in the case of the first three, the task to which that particular kind of reading is suited.

Table 2: Four reading strategies

Strategy	Task to which this strategy is suited
'Exploratory' reading	Summarizing a publication, gaining an overall appreciation – a bird's-eye view – of it.
'Dedicated' reading	Working your way through a book (e.g. a set text) which you have to master if you are to do well in your exam.
'Targeted' reading	Finding something specific, e.g. material to use for an essay, report or dissertation, preparing a presentation, or revising for an exam.
'Can't stop/won't stop' reading (compulsive reading, an involuntary strategy)	If you pick up a book and become so engrossed in it that you can't put it down until you reach the end, it will probably feel more like fun than a task. It won't call for conscious effort, but it may take up a fair amount of time.

It may be that you are sometimes so grabbed by something you're reading that you just can't put it down, and don't want to even though it's three in the morning. I won't tell you to resist that compulsion. But you have a lot of work to do, and you must make best use of your limited time. Accordingly this guide concentrates on exploratory, dedicated and targeted reading. If there's a book that really grabs you, and you want to read it just for interest and pleasure, save it as a treat: make it a reward for yourself when you've completed an essay or given a presentation.

Making notes and translating 'academic-speak'

Before tackling reading strategies, there are some general points I want to put to you.

First, as far as note-taking is concerned, please resist any urge you might feel to copy out word for word, by hand, large chunks of a book. By doing this you are merely acting as a highly inefficient copying machine. Worse, the material is still the property of the author, so to speak: it hasn't passed through your mind and been mentally digested by you. It isn't 'yours'. Mere copying out is intellectually worthless.

Second, try not to spend hours condensing passages from books. If you do this without any sense of what is relevant among the material, you are again – in my view – largely wasting your time. Condensing is a plodding, brute-force approach to reading matter. It's like looking for pearls by crushing oysters into small bits. Instead, be selective. Look for the two or three 'learning points' to take away with you, make a list of the author's main conclusions, capture the 'method, observations, conclusions' or whatever. And don't forget to note where you found these gems, so you can find them again later if you need to.

Third, don't despair if what you find in a book contradicts what you already know, or had thought you knew. If you have made a mistake, this is an opportunity to clear the matter up, and when you have done so you will know this bit of your subject better than before. And sometimes you will find a genuine disagreement between authors. Excellent! This is an opportunity to learn the skill of critical reading. Try to track down the source of the disagreement. Is it a difference in assumptions? Or in the data used? Or in methods of analysis? And when you have tracked down the source of the disagreement, try to form your own judgment as to who is right. Judge for yourself if someone has made an unwarranted inference or logical error. If you're not confident about this, ask your teachers for help. They should be intrigued by problems like these that involve detective work.

Don't expect critical reading to come easily. It takes experience. Finding and reading books by more than one author on the same subject and exploring the disagreements between them is a good way of gaining that experience.

Fourth, if you're starting a new subject you'll certainly find it reassuring to have a textbook that covers the whole course, or – failing that – to be pointed to a short introductory book or a review article or two. That's OK for starters, but such 'potted' treatments do little to help you to develop your reasoning in the subject, and in many cases they are inadequate as sources of quotations. So get into the habit of checking out the original sources that they draw on. Apart from anything else, this will help to alert you to the limitations and deficiencies that are to be found in secondary sources, and thereby further develop your critical reading skills.

Fifth, don't expect academic books and articles to be easy to understand when you first open them and start reading. Remember that they are written in 'academic-speak', effectively a foreign language that you will have to translate into language you can understand. If your first language is not English, translating English-language academic-speak will be particularly difficult at first. But don't be disheartened, and don't let the author make you feel stupid or inadequate. Follow the suggestions in this guide, and bit by bit you will achieve mastery.

Sixth, it is always worthwhile to check out the structure of a publication. Not long ago, a student showed me an article which he had been struggling to understand. A quick inspection revealed that there was a statement of the article's aims in the abstract; another, *different*, statement of aims in the introduction; and a third statement of aims, *different again*, in the conclusions. And while the title of the article posed a question, the conclusions did not contain the answer to it! It was not surprising that the student had been struggling to understand the article. His difficulty didn't arise from lack of ability on his part: it arose because the article was a poor piece of work. If you are told to read something which you find to be as badly organized as this example, go back to your teacher and ask: What are the two or three learning points that I should take from this? If you don't get a helpful answer, it may be best to spend no more time on it.

Seventh, my attitude to academic reading is that what you need is an eye for relevance and the ability to translate and make sense of what you read. Speed is not crucial: 100 per cent comprehension of important material *is*.

A word here about 'speed reading' and 'photo-reading' techniques. 'Speed reading' and 'photo-reading' are not reading in the sense that you are accustomed to, a speeded-up version of what you normally do. They are techniques for mentally photographing pages of print – installing them in your subconscious mind – and accessing relevant material on demand. The reading strategies that I advocate in this book do make some use of them – the books that I have drawn on are listed in the 'Further reading' section – but because I have found them of limited help when it comes to translating and comprehending academic-speak I have made some adaptations.

But you may have some bad reading habits that slow you down. If you read aloud, or voice the words under your breath, you are limiting your reading speed to your speaking speed, which is far slower. And if you focus on one word at a time, your eyes are moving along each line of text in a series of jumps rather than smoothly. Speed reading techniques can help you get out of these bad habits. Use any internet search engine to look for 'speed reading' and check out the various systems – starting with those offering free trials – for one that you feel comfortable with. Such techniques may give your eyes some useful training, so that you 'see' two or three lines at a time, rather than focusing on one word, then the next, then the next, and so on.

Eighth, a word of warning about 'course packs'. You may be able to buy – or even be given – a collection of offprints, usually photocopied articles and chapters from books. Be very wary about relying on the latter. A 'middle' chapter from a book, unless it is a 'free-standing' chapter from an edited book, has been taken out of context, and you may be missing a great deal by not seeing that context. So if you're told such a chapter is important to read, look for the book itself and look through at least the first and last chapters. In my experience, students who have done that have almost always found it worthwhile.

Exploratory reading: How to summarize a publication

'Exploratory' reading is what you do if you want to summarize a book, chapter or article; to gain an overall appreciation – a bird's eye view – of it. It's like making a map of a wood without recording every tree in it. It's a helpful thing to do when you're starting out in a new field of study, or if your teacher has asked you to write a review of a book that's new to you.

A good way of getting an overview of a publication – whether it is a 'unitary' book (written as a whole), a self-contained chapter contributed to an edited book, or an article in a journal – is to follow the steps set out in Table 3.

Table 3: Six steps in summarizing

Step	Task
Step 1	See what type of publication you are faced with
Step 2	Get acquainted with the structure of the publication
Step 3	Find out what you can about the author's approach
Step 4	Find out what you can about the author's conclusions
Step 5	'Map' the publication (optional)
Step 6	Compile your summary

Step 1: See what type of publication you are faced with

When you first open something you haven't read before, it is always a good idea to try to get some idea of the *type* of publication it is. In Table 4 I have listed some of the commonly encountered types (and you can see what I mean by 'type' from the contents of the list) together with some key words which will help you to recognize them.

So what should you do? If the publication is a book, take a look through the foreword (if there is one), the preface (if there is one), the introduction and/or Chapter 1, and the final chapter. In the case of a self-contained chapter or article, check out the abstract, the opening section and the concluding section. Don't actually read this material: instead, just run your eyes over it, keeping a lookout for the key words listed in the right-hand column of Table 4. It won't take a lot of practice before you'll be able to tell at a glance what type of publication you're looking at.

Table 4: Types of publication

Type	Brief description	Key words
'Q to A' (Question to Answer)	Starts with a question and concludes with the answer to it. Answers range from plausible speculation to rigorous explanation in terms of theories and mechanisms.	Question, answer, reasoning; puzzle, solution; phenomenon, situation, event, behaviour; explain, explanation, account for, evidence, observations, factors, conditions; process, mechanism; theory.
Research report	The story of what the author did and found.	Investigation, case study, objective, hypothesis; methodology, analysis, evidence, facts, results, findings, significance, conclusions.
Review	Reviews research findings, literature, 'state of the art', current debate, etc., in a field.	Review, literature review, survey, 'state of the art', debate, critique.
Theory	Presents a conceptual framework of some kind and its implications.	Theory, concept, assumptions, model, variables, cause-and-effect, -isms.
Argument	Argues/puts the case for a particular point of view.	Argue, argument, thesis, case, proposition; attack, critique; objections, refutations; valid, invalid, correct, incorrect.
Issue-centred	Starts with an issue (a 'What should be done?' question) and usually concludes by advocating a particular course of action.	Issue, problem, question, dilemma, difficulty; solution, proposal, recommendation, course of action. Should, ought, must; right, wrong; costs, benefits; beneficial, harmful; appropriate, inappropriate.
Thematic	Is constructed around a 'theme', and incorporates elements of some or all of the above.	Theme, aspects, look at, discuss, consider; a contribution to the debate.

Type	Brief description	Key words
Sequence	Contains elements of some or all of the above in a comprehensible sequence.	
Textbook	Contains elements of some or all of the above, especially survey and theory, tailored to a student readership.	

One incidental benefit of this exercise is that you will quickly realize that most if not all of the items on your reading lists were not written for you. For your particular needs, you will require to pay attention to only a limited range of extracts. This will provide some reassurance when you come to grapple with the academic-speak in those items.

Step 2: Get acquainted with the structure of the publication

By the 'structure' of the publication I mean the way it is organized, laid out. To get acquainted with it, here are some questions to ask yourself, and some suggestions for things you can do:

- If the publication is a book, take a look at the contents page or pages. How informative are the chapter headings? How much do they tell you? Are the chapters grouped into 'Parts', and do these have helpful headings?

- Turn to the preface (if there is one) and/or the introduction (which may or may not be labelled Chapter 1) and look for descriptions of what's in the individual chapters. Look out for expressions such as 'In Chapter 2 I examine ...' and 'The third chapter deals with ...'. Then check these against the chapter headings in the contents list. Do this by writing out the contents list, or by making a photocopy, and annotating it, to give yourself a list of chapters with fuller descriptions than the contents page provides.

  N.B. The habit of cross-checking, which encompasses cross-referencing and testing for consistency, is one of the most useful habits that you can

develop as a reader. If you detect inconsistencies (including inconsistencies of vocabulary), be very, very wary. If you can't trust the author
to write clearly, you can't trust him or her to think clearly either.

- Are the chapters split into sections, and – if so – are the headings of the
sections shown in the contents list? If they aren't, go through the
chapters one by one, making your own contents list for each. Simple to
do, but it can be very revealing.

- If the publication is a self-contained chapter or an article, it won't have a
contents list. So it is particularly important that you make your own. Go
through it making a list of headings, subheadings and sub-subheadings.
I'd be surprised if you don't find this extremely helpful. For example,
you may be able to see immediately which sections you should read first
and which you can save for later.

- Where are the publication's conclusions? Is there actually a chapter or
section called 'Conclusions'? If not, and there often isn't, you have to
play a game called 'hunt the conclusions'. They might be in the final
sections of intermediate chapters; or they might be in the preface or
introduction (this is especially likely if the publication is of the theory or
argument type).

- Look for links between chapters and sections. A good place to look is the
first and last paragraphs. In the first paragraph, what you should look for
is a form of words like: 'In the previous chapter/section we saw ...' In the
last paragraph, look for a form of words like: 'In the next chapter/section
...' When you come to the final chapter of a book, skim through it
looking for references to previous chapters. If there are none, you really
should ask what the connection is between that chapter and the earlier
ones.

Step 3: Find out what you can about the author's approach

Begin by reminding yourself what type of publication it is that you're
working on (see Table 4). Then, if the publication is a book, take a closer look
this time at the foreword, preface, introduction and/or Chapter 1, and the
final chapter. In the case of a self-contained chapter or article, take a closer

look at the abstract, the opening section and the concluding section. Then do the following:

- Ask yourself: What is this book for? Who is it for? Indeed, why did the author take the trouble to write it?

- Look for statements of purpose or objectives and check whether they are consistent with one another. Pay particular attention not only to the earlier chapters or sections but also to the concluding ones: it is quite usual to find objectives restated in a book's final chapter or an article's final section, and they may take a form that is different from earlier statements. (Often it's here that you'll find the clearest and most succinct description of authors' objectives, possibly because it was only when they came to write their conclusions that they had fully clarified what they were doing.)

- With a publication of the 'Q to A' type, make a note of the question(s) and the answer(s). Note the event, situation, behaviour that the question refers to, and the mode of reasoning used to get from question to answer. Does the author tell a story, refer to 'factors', use 'counterfactual' ('what if?') reasoning? Does the answer have to be plausible? Or does the author attempt a rigorous explanation, exposing the mechanisms at work and citing consistency with evidence and theory as the test of a good answer? Look carefully at the language the author uses.

- With an 'account of research', write a short note listing the author's objectives, methodology (method of working), results/findings, and conclusions. There are two points to make here: (1) Conclusions are almost always based on an interpretation of results, so look closely at how the author has done this interpreting; and (2) Exploratory reading doesn't require you to have a detailed grasp of the author's methodology, so don't spend a lot of time on this unless you are told to.

- With a publication of the 'review' type, exploratory reading will usually require you to do no more than gain a grasp of the author's conclusions. So I suggest you don't read anything else, unless, again, you are told to, in which case ask: 'Why?'

- With a publication that presents a 'theory', your first task must be to make sure you understand the language used. If you aren't already familiar with it, make a little glossary – a list of words and their meanings

– for yourself. With a book, go through the index at the back, identify terms (words and phrases) that you're not familiar with, and look up their meanings. That done, there are three useful questions you can ask for the purpose of exploratory reading: (a) What does the author say this theory, model or whatever does? (Look for the words 'explain', 'connect', 'integrate', 'relate', 'describe'.) (b) What does the author say about the assumptions or premises on which the theory is based? (c) What does the author say about how the validity and usefulness of the theory can be tested?

- A publication of the 'argument' type will usually start by setting out the point over which there is debate or disagreement, or the position which is being attacked, and the author's own position. The remainder will often take a series of grounds for disagreement, one by one. Note the author's own position and his or her grounds for disagreeing with others.

- With a publication of the 'issue-centred' type, there are several things to do. Look for a clear statement of the issue: this may be buried in a review of the history or literature, and need to be unearthed. Get clear in your mind what the 'solution' is that the author is advocating. Look for assumptions on which the solution is based: these often need to be unearthed, but may well be open to questioning. Find the 'imperative' words ('should', 'ought', 'must', etc.) and the 'value judgment' words ('good', 'bad', etc.) and note whether these occur throughout or only towards the end in deriving the solution.

- With a publication of the 'thematic' type, you may well feel that you're looking at a collage, a patchwork of bits and pieces of 'pure' elements: 'Q to A', explanation, account of research, and so on. Publications of this type, especially books, can be very difficult to get your head round. They're rather like a chest of drawers into which clothes have been stuffed without being sorted. The very language used is often 'high' academic-speak: 'woolly' and unspecific. Characteristically, themes are not stated with the clarity and precision of a question, a phenomenon or a proposition. And authors use terms such as 'look at', 'discuss' and 'consider' rather than 'ask' and 'test'. The only guide you have to the author's approach is the chapter headings and what he or she tells you about their approach in the introductory and concluding chapters/sections.

If you're lucky the heading to a chapter will tell you which particular aspect of the theme is dealt with in that chapter. If you aren't lucky, and the headings are quirky, metaphorical or non-existent (e.g. the chapters are distinguished only by numbers), read the first and last paragraphs for clues as to the subject matter of the chapter. And see what you can glean from reading through the index, if there is one. Terms with the largest number of page entries, whether these cluster together or are widely spread, may well be the themes that have preoccupied the author.

- With a publication of the 'sequence' type, you should find it fairly straightforward to pick out the respective elements. Something like 'survey', followed by 'account of research', followed by 'advocacy', is not uncommon. Pick out the sequence of elements, then tackle them in the ways shown above.

- In a well-organized 'textbook', irrespective of the elements that it contains, you should find informative chapter headings and the structure of the book already mapped out for you. You may be expected to work steadily through the book from beginning to end, or to use it as a reference book, cross-checking with material that you get in lectures. If it is not already done for you, list the chapter subheadings as well as the headings themselves, and make sure you know what each refers to. That will often be sufficient for exploratory reading.

Step 4: Find out what you can about the author's conclusions

Conclusions can take many forms. For example, the conclusions to a research report could include the explanation put forward for the author's findings, a statement about the need for further research, reflections on the methodology employed, and a discussion of the significance and wider implications of the findings. Having tracked down the author's conclusions, ask yourself:

- What kinds of conclusions did the author reach? What are they about? Do I really need to know about all of them? If the answer is 'no', asking this question could save you quite a lot of work.

Incidentally, don't have any qualms about skipping to the final chapter or chapters without first reading the intervening ones. You are under absolutely no obligation to plough through the whole thing. Unless the book is a novel, it really isn't cheating to look at the ending. Indeed, the end of a book is usually a brilliant vantage point for looking back and picking out the author's train of thought.

● If the conclusions are scattered through the publication, when viewed together are they consistent with one another?

● How do the author's conclusions relate to the objectives set out in the preface, introduction or Chapter 1 (in the case of a book) or in the abstract and opening section in the case of a chapter or article? For example, if the author started off with a question, does he or she conclude by restating that question and providing the answer? If the book was intended to be a survey of a field, does the final chapter present an overview? If the article was intended to be a discussion of a theme, does the final section bring different aspects together and present a coherent summing-up?

Note that not all publications have conclusions. This is particularly likely for the 'theory' and 'thematic' types, some of which may strike you – as they do me – as barely structured outpourings of the author's mind. If you have been struggling with a book (say) of this kind, try this. Without looking at it, sit yourself somewhere comfortable, imagine you're having a coffee with a friend, and imagine that your friend is asking you: 'What do you think are the two or three main points that it's worth taking from this book?' Don't stress yourself: just relax, take a clean sheet of paper, and write down whatever comes into your head. (This will probably work even better if you really do go and have coffee with a friend and your friend really does ask you that question!) Then go and see the teacher who recommended the book to you, and ask him or her the same question. The fact that you have made an effort may be conducive to getting a helpful answer.

Step 5: 'Map' the publication (optional)

Mapping is about identifying for yourself the various parts or 'building blocks' of the publication and the links – the connections – between those building blocks, and showing the blocks and the connections in diagrammatic form. Many people find such diagrams helpful, but not everybody does. If you feel that you belong to the latter group, feel free to skip this step.

You have already done some of this work in Steps 1–4, when you familiarized yourself with the publication's type and layout and found out what you could about the author's approach. Now it's time to concentrate on the links.

To start, take as blocks the chapters and/or sections, i.e. blocks as the author has created them. A link exists between two such blocks when the later one *draws on* the earlier one in some way or is a *logical sequel* to it. Thus in an account of research framed to test an hypothesis, you will almost certainly find that the description of the work carried out draws on the hypothesis formulated in an earlier chapter, that the report of the results *refers back* to the description of the work carried out, that when discussing the significance of results the author *picked out* certain of those results.

In effect, what we are doing here is describing the links between blocks in terms of a *physical action or relationship* of some kind. Here are some more examples:

- The methodology *is based on* the hypothesis that ...
- In the conclusions, the author returns to the question posed at the outset, so the book *comes full circle* ...
- The discussion *brings together* ...
- These assumptions *lead to* the conclusion that ...
- There are three *successive stages* in the author's argument ...
- Each of the case studies *is self-contained* ...

With a little bit of practice it should be fairly straightforward to show in diagrammatic form each of the relationships or dynamics that you find. Lines, arrow-heads and boxes are the only tools you need.

Get yourself a large sheet of paper: flipchart paper is the best, whichever way up you prefer. (Experiment with both 'portrait' and 'landscape'.) Start with a rough draft. Pick out any sequence of blocks that seems to be obvious and draw connecting lines between them to represent the links: this will give you a kind of 'spine' to your map. Then work out how the other blocks connect (or don't) to this spine. Put in each link by drawing a line between the two connected blocks. Carry on doing this until all the links that you have identified are shown. If there are any unconnected blocks left, show these by 'islands' around the edge of your sheet of paper. When all the blocks and links are shown, hey presto! You have your map!

The 'shape' of your map has some important messages for you. If it consists entirely of islands, don't waste your time trying to invent links (but do check with your teacher in case you have overlooked something important, and while you're about it ask why this book has been commended to you). If there are just a few islands, those blocks are evidently not part of the 'mainstream' of the author's exposition, and for the purposes of exploratory reading you can probably safely ignore them.

Sometimes you will also see that certain parts of the book did *not* contribute to the conclusions – they aren't actually mentioned in the final chapter – and you will be able to ignore these deviations or leave them until later.

If your map is basically a line of links – a chain of blocks from 'background' to 'conclusion', let's say – with other links connecting to blocks at the sides, you need to use arrows to show whether those blocks are 'feeding in' to the main chain or 'branching off'. If the latter, note their presence, but don't pay too much attention to them. They are literally side-issues. Concentrate on the main chain and the blocks that feed in to it.

Occasionally you may find that some of your links form a 'loop', with the arrow-heads all pointing clockwise or anti-clockwise. This may indicate that you are being admitted to the author's thought processes. Bear in mind that in writing a book an author is constrained by two needs: the need to force his or her material into a linear, chapter-by-chapter progression, and the need to present it in a way that the reader can assimilate. If the book is an original piece of work, you can be absolutely certain that the author's thought process was complicated and far from linear: more akin to doing a jigsaw puzzle where the picture is blurred, many of the pieces are missing, and there are no straight edges or right-angled corners. (Any academic book that conceals this amounts to fiction as far as the author's thought process is concerned, and you should treat it as such.) So loops in your map may be interesting to pursue later.

Finally: mapping a book is a good way of 'capturing' on a single sheet of paper what the author is presenting and – more important – those blocks that will be of relevance to you in your studies. The map is also a visual aid:

preparing it and subsequently looking at it will help to fix your overview of the book in your memory. With practice, you should be able to create a map of a book of 250 pages in 30 or 40 minutes and form your own view of its value to you.

Step 6: Compile your summary

Compiling your summary is basically a matter of putting together – assembling – the notes you made in steps 1–4, possibly adding any thoughts that have occurred to you while making your map. So it could be divided into five sections:

- Type of publication: give factual details (e.g. title, author, date of publication, publisher), note its type from Table 4, and add any thoughts you've had about it.

- Structure of the publication: describe briefly how it is organized – how it is divided into parts and how they fit together. Your map will come in useful here. Comment on how easy (or not) you found it to grasp the structure, and on any complications or omissions you have found.

- The author's approach: say what you have discovered about the author's objectives and methods, and again add any relevant comments you may have, including a comment as to whether it is suited to the audience for which the author intended it.

- The author's conclusions: again, say what you have discovered. Refer back to Step 4 for the points you could include here.

- The main points that you take from the publication, and how it helps you in studying the subject.

Dedicated reading: How to make the material 'yours'

Dedicated reading builds on exploratory reading, and takes you further into the material. Dedicated reading is called for where you have to master a publication, so your special goal is to make the material 'yours'. In this state, you will feel that you 'know' the material. You will be able to describe accurately the thinking and the methods that the author used, and to identify their strengths and weaknesses. You will be able to use his or her language fluently, and translate it.

To attain this goal, it will be extremely helpful to you – indeed, it's really a necessity – to have your own copy of the book or a photocopy of the chapter or article. You should also be prepared to write in the book: if you're unhappy about doing this, try to bring yourself to use a soft (2B) pencil so you can easily erase notes and markings later. Even if you only put sidelines in the margin, this does help you to make the material 'yours'.

Here are some things to do:

- Do an exploratory read first, using the suggestions in the previous chapter.

- Make a habit of looking through the book or whatever regularly. It will become less intimidating as you become more familiar with it: you reach a point where you can open it at any page and recognize immediately the words or diagrams, figures, tables etc. that you see in front of you.

- If the book has a full contents list – i.e. not only chapter headings but subheadings (section headings) too – make a photocopy of it. If it doesn't have a full contents list, go through it and compile your own. On your list, tick off the chapters and sections that you feel you understand and don't have a problem with. 'Prioritize' those you still have to get to grips with, i.e. decide the order you're going to tackle them in.

- Get to work on your top priority chapter or section. See if there's anything in it you can ignore for the moment (e.g. fine detail, examples, side-issues, commentary, discussion of other writers' work), and bracket [ ] these bits off.

- Now actual work can be delayed no longer. Take the first sentence of the passages that remain. Do you understand it? If it seems complicated, see if you can break it down into two or more short sentences: the shorter the better. Now paraphrase each sentence: express it differently in your own words, in language you can understand.

  This exercise should reveal to you any terms – words or expressions – whose meaning isn't clear to you. It's crucial that you master these. Remember that you're dealing with academic-speak, a foreign language. So make your own mini-dictionary/phrasebook for the subject. When you come across a word, expression, sentence, diagram or whatever that you don't immediately understand, puzzle out its meaning – which means translating it into language that you *do* understand. Look it up in other books, perhaps, or ask your teacher for help. Then write it down on a sheet of punched paper, so you now have a note of its meaning, and/or examples of how to use the term, for your own use. Put the sheet in a ring binder. You have started your mini-dictionary.

  Once you've started your own mini-dictionary, keep a lookout for different definitions of the same word. This will tell you that you're in a field where different writers may use the same word to mean different things: that's to say, you're dealing with meanings rather than standard definitions. It's important to be aware of this. You can extend your mini-dictionary by adding sheets on the concepts, theories, other authors etc. that you encounter in the book. Don't forget to note the numbers of the pages where you found them.

You might find it useful to take this idea further and create your own 'user manual' for each of the courses that you are taking, incorporating your mini-dictionary, lecture notes and handouts, worked examples and problems, past exam papers, reading lists and essay topics, and any other material that comes your way.

Note that for some subjects you may need a multiple dictionary. For example, in the case of economics you may need a four-column dictionary: ordinary English; economics-speak; diagrams; equations.

- Work your way steadily through the significant passages in the book. Gradually you'll find that the passages you don't understand are reduced to little islands in the publication. With the bulk of it under your belt, you can then polish these off one by one.

- Cross-check all your material. Look up in other books or your lecture notes the words, concepts, theories, authors that you found in your first book and included in your mini-dictionary. Sometimes what you find will confirm what you already knew; often it will extend your knowledge or provoke you to further thoughts, and so enable you to make useful additions to your user manual. Cross-checking like this will broaden your knowledge and deepen your understanding and help the material to stick in your mind. At this stage you are thoroughly engaging with the subject, and you'll find that writing in your own words – rather than simply quoting or paraphrasing the writers you've encountered – is beginning to come easily to you. I promise!

Part Three

Targeted reading

The principle behind targeted reading

For much of your time at university, the pattern of your life will be governed by 'deadlines' by which essays have to be handed in and class or seminar presentations delivered. Consequently, you have the task of finding and extracting from the literature material that is relevant to your particular topic, and then of putting the extracts and your own ideas together in a logical, interesting and cogent way for your essay or presentation or whatever, all within a tightly constrained period of time. This calls for 'targeted' reading.

The task of targeted reading has two main parts: identifying key terms (words and expressions) and scanning for relevant material. The next two sections deal with these in turn.

The principle behind targeted reading is that you read *selectively*, to find passages that are *relevant* to your needs. Please remember: *relevance is the key!* It is not – I repeat, not! – necessary that you follow the author's thoughts sentence by sentence, paragraph by paragraph and chapter by chapter. You don't read by starting at page 1 and going on, page by page, until you get to the end. *You look for what you want!* So you start by identifying key terms and carefully scrutinizing your reading list. You then *scan* books, articles and chapters to find these key terms. This should lead you directly to that relevant material.

Remember that the author was not writing for *you*, or to enable you to write your particular essay. The author may have had very good reasons for presenting his or her material in a certain way, but that does not mean that you have to swallow it whole. Instead, your 'reading mission' is a kind of 'treasure hunt': you have to find those precious 'nuggets' that you need for your essay, the bits that are relevant to your task.

Fortunately, a treasure hunt is the kind of task that most people's brains enjoy. In contrast, there are few bigger turn-offs for a brain than being asked to absorb a mountain of words! If, like most people, you have had the experience of your mind wandering and day-dreaming when you have tried to force it to soak up pages and pages of stuff, please remember that this is your brain's strategy for preserving itself from ridiculous pressure. Almost certainly, you were reading without having a reasonably clear idea of what you have been looking for, without being able to recognize what is relevant (that word again!) in the pages in front of you. And in effect, your brain was sending you a message, which is, to put it simply: *You are giving me a really hard time! Do not make me do this!*

And *my* message to you is: preserve your sanity! Pay attention to what your brain is telling you! If reading becomes a chore, ask yourself: what am I looking for?

One final point, which relates to the arrangement of this book. To make it more readable than it otherwise would be, and to help you to find your way round it, I have separated reading from writing. As you see, this part of the book deals with reading, the next with writing. *You do not have to divide up your own reading and writing in this way.* Of course, it may sometimes suit you to do all the reading first, then put your books to one side and write the essay all in one go. You have everything you need in your head: all you are doing now is assembling the essay on paper or the screen. But at other times you will get started on your essay and then find you want to look things up, as fresh ideas occur to you. That's because writing is helping you to think, to crystallize your ideas and come up with new ones. This is 'writing as (an aid to) thinking' as opposed to 'writing as assembly job'.

If you're operating in 'writing as thinking' mode, it is absolutely fine to 'interleave' your reading and writing. For example, you might want and be able to draw up a rough essay plan before doing any reading at all. Then, while you're reading, every now and again you'll return to the plan and refine it or reorganize it. Or you may want to get started and write as much as you can, and then go off to read to fill in the gaps that remain. *There is no single correct way of doing it.* Go about your task in whatever way feels comfortable to you and best suited to you and the particular task you're engaged on.

How to identify key terms

Before you can begin your treasure hunt for those precious 'nuggets', you have to be clear what you are looking for, what will be relevant to your task. Your starting point will be the topic which you have chosen or which has been assigned to you.

I expect you already know about topics. They come in a variety of forms:

The direct question: a sentence with a question mark [?] at the end.

The statement: a proposition or assertion in quotation marks [' '] followed by the instruction 'Discuss' or one of its variants (e.g. 'Discuss critically', 'Do you agree?') or a sentence beginning 'Consider the view that ...'.

The subject: You're merely told 'Write about ...'.

The task: You're instructed to do something, such as 'Describe ...',

'Identify ...', 'Compare and contrast ...', 'Carefully explain ...', 'Critically evaluate ...'.

The problem: You're expected to apply techniques and reasoning to the data given to arrive at a solution.

If you're given just the subject it won't be apparent when you first look at it what you are expected to do. This may well also be the case with a question or a statement. So you will have to clarify it and identify the key terms, i.e. the key words and expressions.

How to do this? Here are some suggestions. Look at the actual words and expressions in the topic, and make a note of the following:

- Those words and expressions that you think have a particular significance in the subject that you're studying.

- The *phenomena* (including events and situations), the *themes* or the *issues* that are mentioned in the topic.

- The names (of people, places etc.) that are mentioned.

- Any systems, structures, relationships (especially cause-and-effect ones) and/or processes that are mentioned or implied.

- Any categories or classes mentioned.

- Any theories, propositions, concepts and ideas mentioned.

- The names of any writers mentioned.

- Any specialized terms mentioned if you haven't already included them under another heading. (For example, for a law topic these would include statutes and cases.)

As a safeguard, ask yourself whether there are other key terms that you should also make a note of even though they are not specifically mentioned in the topic. For example, is there a particular writer or a particular concept you need to cover? Look at your lecture handouts, reading lists and any notes that you have, and pick out these extra key terms and add them to your list.

Finally, look at past exam papers and see if there are other key terms that tend to be associated in exam topics with those you've already identified. If there are, add these others.

You now have a list of key terms. Most of them should be specific enough to be found in the index of a book on the subject.

Your list needs to be short and manageable. If it's a long list, look for ways of shortening it. Perhaps it could be divided into a short essential list and an additional list. If some of the terms seem too general, look for more specific ones to replace them with. The 'treasure' that you'll be looking for consists of references to, and discussion of, these terms in the books, chapters and articles that have been recommended to you.

Box 1

How to use a reading list

First of all, please reread 'Coping with monster reading lists', pages 15–16. This should help you not to be intimidated by the length of a list and give you a start in focusing on what you actually need.

What should you do with your reading list? First, you should do the obvious thing. Look to see how much guidance it gives you. If good practice has been followed, you should be able to answer 'Yes' to all the following questions:

- Has your teacher 'starred' any items as essential reading, or divided the list into two parts, such as 'Main reading' and 'Further reading', or books and articles?
- Are particular chapters or pages recommended?
- Does the list give the year of publication of books?
- If books are collections of articles by different people – these books should be shown as having editors rather than authors – have particular chapters been picked out as more relevant to your needs?

Now start your search with essential or main reading, and with the most recent items: these are most likely to give you an overview of the subject and to have the fullest range of further references to follow up. Even if a book that you need is being used by someone else, go to the shelf where it should be and see if there are other books nearby that you can use.

Get hold of as many books and articles as you can.

How to scan a book

When you first look at a book, your task is *not* to start reading it through but to seek out and discover where the bits you want are to be found: the chapters, the sections, the pages, the paragraphs that are relevant to your needs because they deal with the key terms that you have identified. This process of seeking out and discovering relevant extracts is what I mean by 'scanning'.

In this section I deal primarily with 'unitary' books, i.e. ones that are written as a whole by one or (sometimes) two authors. There is another category of books, namely edited books that consist of a collection of chapters by a number of authors. These chapters in edited books have to be considered individually, like articles in journals, and I cover this too.

I suggest that you adopt the following procedure. You will need to have by you some sheets of A4 paper and a large stack of Post-its: 5 inches by 3 inches (approx. 13cm x 8cm) is the most convenient size, and you might like to have them in a range of colours. The idea is to use them as bookmarks.

Table 5 sets out the seven steps in scanning a book.

Table 5: Seven steps in scanning

Step	Task
Step 1	Remind yourself of your key terms
Step 2	Scan the contents page
Step 3	Scan the index
Step 4	More bookmarks
Step 5	Scan the whole book
Step 6	Photocopy the most important bits (optional but recommended)
Step 7	Organize and apply your results

Step 1: Remind yourself of your key terms

Write or type out your list of key terms, in large print, on a piece of paper with nothing else on it. Ideally, use colours or highlighter to make the words stand out. Read the list aloud half-a-dozen times (quietly if you're in the library), and move a finger down the list each time as you do so. All this is to prime your mind for the search you're about to make.

Step 2: Scan the contents page

Open the book at the contents page (the list of chapters), and look down the page to see if one of your key terms is actually a chapter title, or appears in a chapter title. This will take you only a few seconds. If your key term is there, find the start of that chapter and stick a Post-it in there, with the top half or third sticking out above the book, to act as a bookmark. *Do not start reading yet!*

Step 3: Scan the index

Now go to the first page of the index at the back of the book. Run your index (!) finger steadily but quickly down the columns of the index, column by column, and follow your fingertip with your eyes. *Do not read the words that are written there!* If you find yourself reading them, you are either going too slowly, in which case move your finger faster, or you are focusing too hard, in which case relax your eyes and just gaze at the page above your fingertip. If you have primed your mind well, when you get to one of your key terms it will automatically catch your eye. This is exactly what you want to happen! With practice, words and expressions will leap off the page at you.

When one of your key terms catches your eye, take your list of key terms and by that particular one make a note of the page number or numbers (if there's a sequence, e.g. 102–9, note just the first) and then carry on running your finger down the columns until the next key term catches your eye. Again, note the page number(s) and carry on. You should get to the end of the index no more than three or four minutes after you started.

Step 4: More bookmarks

Find each of the pages that you noted in the index exercise that you just did, and stick a Post-it there. If it's the left-hand page of a two-page spread, stick it on the right-hand one, again with part of the Post-it sticking out of the book.

Step 5: Scan the whole book

Look again at your list of key terms, move your finger down the list and read them out loud again, just to remind yourself of them. Now it's time to scan the whole book. Turn to the first page of text. (It may be a preface, or introduction, or Chapter 1.) You're going to do what you did with the index, but because you're working with a page width instead of a column you might like to use two fingers: the index and the middle finger. Move those fingers steadily but quite quickly straight down the middle of the page – first the left-hand page of a two-page spread and then the right-hand page –

and follow your fingertips with your eyes. This should take you no more than a couple of seconds per page. When you get to the foot of the right-hand page, turn over and carry on scanning.

Again, *don't read the sentences yet!* If you find yourself reading the actual words and trying to make sense of them you're either going too slowly: speed up! or you're focusing too hard: relax! (Incidentally, a sign of your eyes being nicely relaxed is that you can see *two* vertical creases between the left- and right-hand pages: the parallax effect.) And don't worry that you might be missing words at the edges of pages (i.e. the beginnings and ends of lines): your peripheral vision will take care of those.

When one of your key terms catches your eye, grab a Post-it and stick it on the page in the usual fashion. Jot down the page number on the Post-it and a brief note of what's there. When you come to a Post-it that you put in earlier, when doing the index exercise, see if there actually is a key term nearby that you can mark with it.

Get to the end of the book as quickly as you can. Around 15 minutes for a 250-page book would be about right. (I'm not joking: remember that what you're doing is *scanning*, not reading as such.)

Do this for all the pieces of reading you're going to use. (Different colour Post-its come in handy to denote different books or articles.) If you are in the habit of reading slowly and carefully in order not to miss anything, you will find it very comforting and reassuring to have these bookmarks.

Step 6: Photocopy the most important bits (optional but recommended)

You now have a book that may be bristling with Post-its. If these cluster together, photocopy those pages and any others needed to complete a chapter or section. (Take care to lift Post-its off pages while you're photo-copying them.)

Step 7: Organize and apply your results

Your final task in the scanning process is that of organizing your work and applying it to your task.

If you are able to hold on to the book for a little while longer, it would be a good idea at this point to spend a little time on appreciating the topic that you have to work on, and creating your plan (see the two sections after the next one, below). It will give you a stronger sense of what bits of the book are relevant if you can see how you would use them in your essay.

If the book you've been using is one that you've borrowed and have to return, go through it, starting at the beginning, finding and retrieving your Post-its one by one. At each one you come to, read the passage referring to your key term and ask yourself whether it is relevant to your task and accordingly worth making a note of. You might consider that the passage is merely a passing reference, or duplicates something better expressed elsewhere, in which case simply remove that Post-it and go on to the next.

When you come to a worthwhile reference, make a note of it. If you are making a mini-dictionary and/or personal user manual for the course, you may want to make some entries in them. Alternatively, make your note on a piece of paper (see below for ideas on making notes) or electronically, or on the Post-it itself. A very brief note will do if the Post-it is on a page that you have photocopied. Make sure the Post-it also has the page number on it, then remove it. Keep doing this until you have removed all of the Post-its from the book.

An optional but neat thing to do with all those Post-its is this. Get yourself a sheet of flip-chart paper and stick the Post-its on to it. Now move them around until related ones are clustered together and, ideally, the clusters themselves are in a logical relationship to one another. Stick the sheet of flip-chart paper on your wall with a piece of Blu-Tack or something similar. You can add further Post-its produced by reading more books or articles, building up your clusters or creating fresh ones, all on the same piece of paper.

When you're happy with the arrangement, you might like to draw lines to connect related clusters.

Doing all this will engage your mind. Sticking up Post-its and moving them around sounds like a simple activity, but it will familiarize you with the material and get you thinking about what clusters with what, and about what relationships and connections you can find. It will also help you to remember what you have been thinking about. If the book you've been using is your own, you might be content to leave the Post-its in place. The important thing is that when you are drafting your essay you know exactly where to find the material you want.

This completes your scan of the book you've been working on. Treat other books in the same way, add the resultant notes and Post-its to your collection, and incorporate them all into your own personal user manual for your course.

Box 2

How to scan an article or chapter

Articles in journals and self-contained chapters in edited collections require a slightly different treatment from 'unitary' books, because they don't have their own list of contents or their own index. An extremely useful thing to do, therefore, is to make your own contents list.

Simply go through the article or chapter and make a list of the headings that you find. Once you have done this you will have the measure of the piece, so to speak, and you will immediately feel much more comfortable and familiar with it.

Having made your own contents list, go through the same steps as for a unitary book.

Again, remember that it will be helpful for you to be in that receptive state of mind where your key terms will jump off the page at you. So once again follow your fingertips steadily down the pages at a speed fast enough for you not to lapse into actual reading.

Part Four

Writing essays

Discovering what's wanted from you

Before you can build the results of your reading into your essay, you must have some sense of what's wanted from you. There are, I suggest, three questions that you need to ask:

- What type of essay is wanted?
- What mindset should I approach it with?
- In what style should I write?

Essay types

Essays, like publications, can be seen to be of different types. I list my version of these types in Table 6, together with samples of the instructions or openings frequently found in the topics set for essays. Not surprisingly, the list is very similar to that in Table 4. Table 6 also gives samples of the instructions that you may come across for each type, both in essay topics set for you and in past exam papers.

Table 6: Essay types and sample instructions

Type	Sample instructions
Basic (definitional, descriptive)	● Define ...
	● What is ...?
	● What is meant/do you understand by ...?
	● Describe ...
	● State the principles ...
	● What are the main features of ...?
	● Compare and contrast ...
	● Outline the method used to ...
	● Give an account of ...
'Q to A' (Question to Answer)	● Why did [a particular event or situation] come about/fail to come about?
	● Why does ...?
	● Account for .../Explain why ...
	● To what extent [did certain factors play a part in] ...?
	● 'X was responsible for ...' Discuss. (The question here is: 'Was X responsible ...?')
	● What are the causes of ...?
	● What mechanism gives rise to ...?
Report on an investigation	● Describe/give an account of an experiment you would carry out/have carried out to ...
	● How would you test the hypothesis that ...?
	● How reliable/significant are the results of ...?
Review	● How comparable are ...?
	● How can we reconcile ...?
	● Review the evidence for ...
	● 'There is widespread agreement/no agreement as to ...' Discuss/do you agree?

Type	Sample instructions
Theory	<ul><li>How does X's theory of ... help us to understand ...?</li><li>Critically evaluate X's theory of ...</li><li>How applicable is ... to ...?</li><li>[Quotation] Discuss/Comment/Do you agree?</li><li>Comment on the view that ...</li><li>Discuss/explore/comment on the assumptions underlying ...</li></ul>
Argument	<ul><li>How well founded is the argument that ...?</li><li>What argument/case can be made for ...?</li><li>[Quotation/statement] Discuss/Comment/Do you agree?/Is this fair comment?</li><li>Comment on the view that ...</li></ul>
Issue-centred	<ul><li>What problems face ...?</li><li>Comment on/how would you evaluate proposals to ...</li><li>How should ...?</li><li>'X can never succeed [unless] ...' Discuss/ comment/do you agree?</li><li>Under what conditions can ...?</li><li>Write a report advising ...</li></ul>
Thematic	Any of the instructions listed above.

Some academics have the regrettable and unhelpful habit of not giving their students a question or instruction: they simply say 'Write about X', which leaves you completely in the dark. If this happens to you, make up your own. Model it on one of those in Table 6 or find one in a past exam paper. Questions are better than instructions. A good question is like a sharp knife: it cuts through assumptions and waffle.

Mindsets

Every academic has a 'mindset': a collection of preconceptions and taken-for-granteds that he or she isn't consciously aware of but which are manifest in everything they say and write. Almost certainly, what your teacher wants from you is an essay that is consistent with this mindset. If you can take on your teacher's mindset when writing an essay, what you're doing is, in effect, writing for them in a language they can understand, which can only help you to get a good grade. So an important part of finding out what your teacher really wants is figuring out his or her mindset.

Figuring out someone else's mindset isn't as difficult as it sounds once you realize what you have to do. And because it involves detective work, doing it can be quite fun. It requires you to pay close attention to your teachers' styles and the very language they use, especially in their lectures and their writings, as well as in the essay topics and exam questions they set. In Table 7 I list the academic mindsets that tend to be associated with particular essay types and offer some suggestions as to what to look for to identify them. Look and listen carefully, and do check out your impressions with your fellow students.

Table 7: Essay types and associated mindsets

Type	Associated mindsets and features to notice
Basic (definitional, descriptive)	Stresses basic stuff that you need to know: factual material, things you can look up. Lectures start from first principles, courses build step by step. They tend to be well organized: your essays should be too.
'Q to A' (Question to Answer)	Lectures and writings open with questions chosen because they are puzzles that have attracted the teacher's interest. They may be of different kinds: not just 'Why did X happen?' but 'Why did it happen where it did/when it did/in the form that it did?' Notice if they supplement these with counterfactual questions: 'rather than at some other time/at some other place/ in some other form?' Notice too how answers to questions are arrived at – e.g. by citing prior events/situations (hence a good deal of narrative), or the conjunction of certain factors, or the writings of other academics – and follow the same pattern in

Type	Associated mindsets and features to notice
	your essays. Notice what counts as a good answer: one that is 'plausible' or 'well argued', perhaps? Notice if a 'good' answer is one that carries authority: 'To me, the weight of evidence clearly supports X's argument.' The crucial words here are 'to me': look out for hints that you contradict at your peril.
	Are lectures and writings aimed at explanation, at uncovering mechanisms and processes? Is consistency with observations (evidence) and theories the aim, rather than mere plausibility? If so, your approach must have these aims too.
Report on an investigation	Notice whether this takes the form of a straightforward, 'linear' progression from the objective of the investigation (could be to test an hypothesis, or to see what happens when ...) through theoretical background, methodology, observations (data collected), findings (analysis of data collected), interpretation/ significance of findings (results), to conclusions. Or does the author omit steps or take them out of their logical sequence? Notice also the steps in which choices are made and judgment exercised, and how self-critical or self-justificatory the presentation is.
Review	Notice whether this is done in a very compartmentalized and/or uncritical way ('X says ...', 'According to Y, ...', 'Let me now turn to Z, ...'). Alternatively, are connections made: contributions put together, similarities and differences highlighted, syntheses made, conclusions drawn?
Theory	Notice how high the level of academic-speak is, and how much name-dropping. Some academics teach as if the literature on the subject were itself the subject. Look out for courses on 'great thinkers' and examination papers consisting largely or entirely of quotations from their works which you are instructed to 'discuss' or 'discuss critically'. You will need to draw heavily on the literature yourself. Notice whether any 'raw' data drawn from the 'real world' are cited. (If not, never ever introduce such material in your essays, especially anything drawn from your personal life experience.)
Argument	Some teachers see their task as one of persuasion. Listen for their use of the words 'argue' and 'argument' – 'In this lecture I

Type	Associated mindsets and features to notice
	shall argue that ...', 'My argument is ...' – and lectures that are essentially attempts to persuade you that their point of view is correct. Notice how they construct their arguments and what kind of material they cite in support of them. Notice too how they deal with material that does not support them (do they ignore it?) and how they treat authors with whom they disagree. If their approach seems sloppy to you, try to do better, but use their language when you can.
Issue-centred	Notice the procedure for getting from the issue – the 'what should be done?' question – to the proposal, usually via formulating alternative courses of action and assessing their actual/likely consequences, then applying value judgments. Again, if their approach seems sloppy to you, try to do better, but use their language when you can.
Thematic	Listen for the words 'theme', 'aspects', 'look at', 'consider'. Try to break down the presentation into component parts. Do these form a logical progression? If not, do they amount to a 'collage', a patchwork of facts, research findings, quotations, critiques, categorizations, opinions, appeals to common sense, etc? Listen out for definitions of terms: these are liable to be all-encompassing and abstract, rather than enabling you to recognize an X when you see it. And notice the use of metaphors, for example in titles like 'Molehills into mountains: a study of the growth of universities.' Yet again, if their approach seems sloppy to you, try to do better, but use their language when you can.

Note: Few academics take exactly the same approach to a subject as their colleagues. So compare the approaches of different teachers, both within and across disciplines. Compare the ways in which they structure lectures, their preferences as to exam questions, how they use published materials. Ask yourself questions like 'Do economists think differently from economic historians?', and then try to put your finger on the differences that you observe. And compare notes with your fellow-students.

Writing styles

One of your tasks as a university student is to carry out your own little research projects to discover what 'writing styles' your teachers like. By 'writing style', I mean the way you organize your essay and present your material. Some examples will make this clearer.

Sometimes a teacher will say he or she wants to see a strong argument, or a personal exploration of ideas, or a step-by-step reasoned answer to a question, or a literature review showing you have read widely and critically. There may be a marking sheet with a list of criteria against which your essay will be assessed: see if you can get hold of a copy before you start writing.

But what does your teacher *really* want? If he or she says they want to see a strong argument, do they mean they want you to state your point of view at the beginning and follow it up with every bit of material (evidence, opinion etc.) you can find that supports your point of view? (In which case, what are you meant to do with any evidence that *doesn't* support your point of view? Ignore it?) Or do they really mean they want an essay from you that is closely reasoned? Which would – to my way of thinking – require you to examine all relevant material and come to a conclusion only after you have done so. If your teacher asks you for a strong argument or something similar, *do ask what he or she means, and what they actually want you to provide.*

Note: Be aware of the mixed messages that you'll get if your essay topic is a question (with a question mark at the end) but you're told by your teacher that he or she wants to see an 'argument'. Answering a question requires you to operate in 'Q to A' mode, reasoning your way from question to answer. But 'arguing', as normally understood, requires you to state your answer at the outset. You cannot do both at once. (An argument is not an answer to a question!) If you try to do both at once, you will scramble your brain: it's a sure-fire recipe for writer's block. I have met many students who have started writing an essay to answer a question with the words 'In this essay I shall argue ...' and then found themselves completely at a loss as to how to continue.

Sadly, I have never met a student who has been told by a teacher: 'This is how we construct an argument in this discipline', let alone 'This is how to argue.' Likewise, I have never met a student who has been told by a teacher: 'This is how to discuss.' *If you have a teacher who wants you to 'argue' or 'discuss', ask him or her how to do it.* Ask to be shown how. Ask where you can find examples. And try to spend some time in lectures simply observing how they themselves do it: notice what counts as argument or discussion for them, and what makes an argument or discussion a good or sound one. (Get one of your friends to take notes during those lectures, and then trade your observations for their notes.) Read and inspect closely anything that they themselves have published.

How to clarify your topic

Before you get down to writing your essay it will greatly help you to have at least a rough plan for it. But before you can produce that plan you need to clarify the topic that you have been set. Most essay topics take the form of a direct question to answer, a statement to discuss, or a task to carry out. (See 'How to identify key terms', pages 46–48.) Direct questions and statements in particular frequently contain traps for the unwary. If you want to produce a good essay it is absolutely crucial that you are aware of these traps, so that you can avoid them. Here are some questions to help you develop this awareness.

● Is it clear to you what the question or statement means, or what the task requires you to do?

If the question or whatever is ambiguous, i.e. it could be interpreted in more than one way, you will need to consider the alternatives and justify your choice in the introduction to your essay. *Never* jump to any conclusion without thinking about what is expected of you.

● Are there words or expressions in the topic that are capable of more than one meaning, or are colloquial, or figures of speech (especially metaphors), and accordingly need to be interpreted?

If you encounter this situation ask your teacher for help. If English is not your first language, consult a native English speaker too. Again, the introduction to your essay would be the appropriate place to discuss how these words or expressions should be interpreted, what meanings should be attached to them. Sometimes you can gain clarity by asking the question: 'How would I recognize X if I saw it?'

● Does the topic include what appears to be a statement of fact (e.g. 'In 1990 there was a change …')?

If so, ask yourself whether this purported fact is accurate? (Was there indeed such a change in 1990?) In your essay you may want to consider what evidence there is that can be used to support or contradict purported facts, and whether some relevant facts have been omitted.

● Are any assumptions implied or stated explicitly in the topic?

You should identify any assumptions that you find and consider and comment on their validity. Can they be tested against evidence?

● Does the topic incorporate reasoning: about cause-and-effect relationships, for example, as in statements of the type 'A led to B'?

If so, consider whether this reasoning too can be tested against evidence.

● Does the topic incorporate any generalized terms or generalizations?

If it incorporates a reference to 'people', say, or 'Europe', you will almost always be expected to break these down: to distinguish between men, women and children in the former case; different countries or groups of countries in the latter. With a generalization of any kind, ask yourself: 'Is this statement always valid? Under what circumstances or conditions is it valid/not valid?'

● Is there a 'hidden' second question or proposition?

With a topic like 'B is the consequence of A: Discuss' be aware of the implied 'hidden' question: 'Is B the consequence of other factors, or of the conjunction of A and other factors?' Be prepared to discuss that possibility. Hardly any phenomena have a single cause.

- Is your instinctive reaction to agree or disagree with the statement or to answer 'yes' or 'no' to the question?

   If so, try to make your thinking explicit, and consider whether there might be certain circumstances under which you would come to a different conclusion.

- Does the topic include the words 'function' or 'role', or other words which could similarly be used in either a descriptive sense ('X performs the function of ...') or a normative sense (implying that 'X ought to ...')?

   If the question or proposition does not make it clear which sense is intended, you should point out and discuss the ambiguity in your introduction. Use of these words in the normative sense also invites you to discuss the matter of who is setting the norms.

- Are any value judgments (crudely, judgments about whether something is good or bad) incorporated in the question or proposition?

   Consider whether the question or statement hinges on such value judgments, and whether people with different perspectives or interests would disagree over it.

- Are you yourself being asked to make a value judgment, e.g. to say whether X was a success or a failure?

   If so, be sure to make clear the criteria you are using: in this case, the criteria by which you are judging success or failure. It may be that X was a success from one point of view (or one group's point of view) and a failure from another. Note that you are being asked not merely to describe the consequences of X: you are being asked to exercise your judgment.

- Is some kind of context – social, political, economic etc. – mentioned in the question or proposition?

   You will usually gain marks for showing that you are aware of the broader context within which it arises. Accordingly you should say whether – in your judgment – it relates to a very special set of circumstances, for example, or to a current contentious issue. Similarly you might point out any wider implications or significance that your answer might have.

- Do any dates, time spans or other time-related words appear in the topic, such as 'today', 'currently', 'always', 'sometimes', 'frequently', 'often', 'rarely', 'recently', 'never'?

These will focus or qualify your answer, and it is crucial that you pay attention to them.

● Are any specialized terms mentioned that you haven't already identified?

Don't overlook these.

● Do the words 'can', 'could', 'may', 'might' appear in the topic?

Be aware that these denote potential – possibility – rather than fact and actuality. You're being asked to consider counterfactuals (alternative 'scenarios'), e.g. what might have happened rather than what actually did.

Box 3

'Basic' essays

'Basic' essays are mostly to do with 'stuff' that you need to know before you can get anywhere in this subject: factual material, definitions, techniques and other things you can look up. The topics are ones that you're likely to be asked to write on at the beginning of a course, to introduce you to the subject and help you get a grounding in it. If you encounter such topics towards the end of a course or in an exam, they are likely to form the first part of a two- (or more) part topic.

Some basic essays are definitional or descriptive. The topics open with instructions or questions like 'Define ...', 'What is ...?', 'What is meant by/do you understand by ...?', 'Describe ...', 'State the principles ...'. Of course, you can always supply what's wanted in a straightforward, matter-of-fact way. But to add value to your essay, see if you can find more than one definition or description, and comment on any discrepancies you find. This will show your teacher that you have thought about what you were doing, not just looked things up mechanically, and I would expect him or her to appreciate this.

With a topic that opens 'What are the main features of ...?', you could just list those features. But to add value, say *why* these features are thought to be 'main' – or major or important or significant – and what distinguishes them from lesser features.

With a 'Compare and contrast ...' topic, again there's a simple thing you could do: just list similarities and differences. To add value in this case, identify and think about the criteria you're using. To give an extremely simple example, if you were comparing butterflies and moths you could write down as a difference that butterflies are active during daylight while moths are active at night. Here the criterion is the level of activity at different levels of natural light.

If you are instructed to 'Outline the method used to ...' or 'Give an account of ...', it will almost certainly benefit you to be as systematic as you can. If the method involves a sequence of steps, make a list of them. If you are giving an historical account, stick to chronological order and/or append a chronology, a list of significant events with dates. Having a chronology is a particularly good idea if your account 'doubles back' in time, e.g. 'King Henry had already, ten years before, ...'.

Thinking it through: a note on methodology

Writing an essay requires you first of all to think through what you are going to do. Once you have clarified your topic, you'll see that if it goes beyond the definitional and descriptive you have to think quite hard about what methodology you will use and what materials you will need.

The notion of 'methodology' (system of methods) is an important one to grasp. You can't *not* have a methodology: that is to say, you will assuredly have one even if you are unaware of it. For example, take the direct question: 'Why did Bismarck resign his position as Chancellor of the German empire in 1890?' Here are four possible methodologies for answering it.

One methodology would be to consult every historian of that era that you can find, so you end up writing an essay about historians' opinions on the subject.

A second methodology would be to narrate (describe) events 'leading up to' his resignation, a methodology which necessitates some judgment on your part as to which prior events were significant and which were not. So you have to ask yourself: How can I tell which prior events were significant and which were not?

A third methodology would be to construct alternative – counterfactual – scenarios. For example, you could ask yourself whether, if Kaiser Wilhelm II had had a different personality, it is likely that events would have followed the same course.

A fourth methodology would be to try to put yourself in Bismarck's position just before he resigned, and ask yourself what alternatives were open to him and how he would have felt about them, so in effect you're trying to reconstruct his rationale.

Note that if you aren't clear what methodology you are using, you run the risk of trying to use two, three or even all four at once, which will thoroughly confuse you. You'll end up submitting an unsatisfactory piece of work – if, indeed, you do succeed in completing it!

So what should you do?

If your topic is in the form of a direct question, ask yourself a further question: *How can I tell?* In the above example, you would ask yourself: How can I tell why Bismarck resigned? Ask yourself what information is available on the subject, and what you could do with it.

If you are instructed to explain a phenomenon, again you must think about *how* to do this. What is the connection between the phenomenon and pre-existing conditions? What is the appropriate way to represent this?

If you are required to make a comparative study of writings in a field you will need first to think about and decide on the criteria you are going to use for your comparison. For example, you might want to make a comprehensive examination of each writer's background, perspective, set of assumptions, objectives, language, and contribution to the advancement of the subject. You might want to identify areas of agreement, and/or you might want to identify disagreements, explore how two or more writers or schools of thought come to different conclusions, and form your own judgment as to which is to be preferred.

If you are required to discuss or comment on a quotation, it would again be advisable to have a clear methodology. You might want to comment on where the writer is 'coming from', which school of thought he or she belongs to, what assumptions or premises the quotation is based on, whether you can detect errors or omissions in the manifest or implied reasoning, the basis of the quotation (for example, is it based on accepted knowledge, empirical observation, theory, appeal to common sense?), the part that value judgments play in it, and so on.

Take particular care when you are writing for a teacher whose style is thematic. It may be difficult to write an essay that is anything more than a string of points loosely connected together: see the next section for ideas on how to do better than this. Thematic teachers are also very prone to use colloquial language. For example, you may be asked to discuss a statement to the effect that such-and-such is 'beyond the pale', or asked the question: 'Does it matter that ...?' 'Beyond the pale' and 'Does it matter?' are colloquial expressions, not technical ones, or ones that you will find defined in academic literature. Consequently you will have to ask 'How can I tell?' when you encounter such language. You will need to 'operationalize' such terms – translate them into terms that will enable you to 'tell' – if you are to write with any intellectual rigour. Although many academics use colloquial language in their lectures and writings without defining their terms, which is not at all helpful to you, if you follow their example your writing is liable to lack structure and precision. This is an instance where it is *not* helpful to follow your teachers' example.

An all-purpose plan

Here are some suggestions for preparing your essay plan. I have tried to make these suggestions 'all-purpose' ones, covering essays of all the types listed in Table 6. All of them entail marshalling relevant materials – 'raw' materials, writings, whatever – giving them your personal treatment, and coming to reasoned conclusions. As I see it, that is what scholarship is all about and that is the business we are all in, teachers and students, whether we see the world in terms of phenomena, arguments, themes or issues.

To begin, have a shot at outlining a plan, a structure, for your essay. This outline plan should take the form of a list of headings and subheadings, or you may prefer to make it a list of bullet points. This first shot need only be tentative. Being able to visualize the essay as a whole early in your writing will help you to judge what to include and what to leave out. Everyone starts with a rough plan and then refines it, so expect your plan to go through several versions.

A generic, all-purpose plan, with main headings and subheadings, is shown in Table 8. You won't need all the subheadings: select the ones that you need and discard the others. For each subheading that you keep, make a short note of what you would cover under that heading, including the key terms that belong there. (The scanning that you have done for your targeted reading will help with this.) Do bear in mind any word limit: the fewer the number of words at your disposal, the more 'telescoped' your plan has to be.

Table 8: An all-purpose essay plan

Heading	Subheadings and content
INTRODUCTION (Every essay needs an introduction.)	(1) Context/background. You may feel it's appropriate to begin by 'setting the scene', showing you're aware of a current debate or issues. If you're absolutely certain it would be relevant and appropriate, you could begin with a quotation.
	(2) Interpretation. Refer back to 'How to clarify your topic', pages 65–69. You will want to say what is meant by any terms that aren't self-explanatory, and to draw attention to anything that a question or statement takes for granted (e.g. implicit assertions and assumptions) and any ambiguities (where the words could have more than one meaning).
	(3) Methodology: a very brief mention. (You'll be giving it a fuller treatment in the methodology section.) A sentence beginning: 'In this essay I shall ...' (or 'This essay will ...' if your teachers don't like essays written in the first person) will usually be sufficient.
	(4) Very brief mention of the materials you're using. A single sentence will usually suffice.
	(5) Outline of what's to come in the following sections. And if your teachers like you to say at the outset what your conclusion will be, a sentence beginning 'It will be concluded/shown/argued that ...' should satisfy them.

Heading	Subheadings and content
METHODOLOGY (You might prefer to give this section the name of the specific technique you're using – e.g. CONTENT ANALYSIS – or just to call it APPROACH.)	(1) Using analytical perspectives. These include concepts, hypotheses, theories and models (and perhaps assumptions), the 'spectacles' through which you view your subject and lead you to regard certain things as significant and others as not. (2) Data processing. Under this heading come whatever techniques of quantitative and qualitative analysis that you are using. (3) Testing against evidence. This involves asking questions such as 'Is this assertion corroborated by the facts?'; 'Is X's hypothesis consistent with the findings of Y's research?'; 'Does this model fit the circumstances?' and 'Have predictions based on this theory been fulfilled by actual events?' (4) Logical testing. This involves questioning the logic of the statement that you are dealing with and scrutinizing the literature for internal inconsistencies, omissions, bias, or defective logic. You might want to check whether the conclusions that someone has drawn from their study do actually follow from the data that they obtained rather than from assumptions they made at the outset. (5) Comparing and contrasting. Be sure to state clearly the criteria that you are using for this exercise. (6) Synthesizing. You might be aiming to put together your own findings with other findings and facts, opinions and hypotheses from a variety of sources, and thereby synthesize an argument of your own. Say so. (7) Evaluation. Say what value judgments (and whose) you are going to base your evaluation on.
MATERIALS USED (Give this section a more descriptive name, e.g. THE CASE STUDIES or LITERATURE REVIEW.)	(1) 'Raw' material, empirical evidence. What data sources, 'facts', records, observations are available to you? What is actually known about this subject? (2) Case studies and other research reports, including inferences drawn by their authors. In addition to citing these, and giving whatever extracts are appropriate, say why you have chosen these particular case studies.

Heading	Subheadings and content
	(3) Reference materials: relevant knowledge and theory. This will include materials of the kind that can be found in textbooks and reference books (e.g. statutes and law reports in the case of law topics). (4) Other literature. This will be a note of other relevant writings that you have read. If you are compiling a literature review, you may want to include short extracts. (Don't copy out long passages: it will not gain you any marks.) Give the gist of what the literature is contributing to your work – concepts to apply, hypotheses to test, questions to answer, disagreements to explore, etc. – but save discussion of it for your 'Discussion' section.
FINDINGS, REASONING, ANALYSIS, and/or RESULTS (Give this section or these sections headings that relate to your specific subject, not these generic headings.)	(1) 'Findings' will be taken directly from your material. (2) 'Reasoning' and 'analysis' are what you do when you apply your methodology to your material. (3) 'Results' are what you get from doing this; they are what you show or demonstrate.
DISCUSSION	If your results fall into a number of parts, or 'strands', your discussion will usually consider them together. It could cover: (1) The validity of your results. What confidence do you have in them? Are they universally valid? How far can one safely generalize from them? Are there particular methodology issues worth mentioning? (2) The implications of your results. These might include (a) their immediate significance; (b) their wider significance, e.g. for future developments in the field; for research; and for the policies and practices of government bodies, non-governmental organizations, and businesses; (c) judgments that you have reached (e.g. of merits and demerits). (3) Comments on and critique of theories, ideas etc. that you encountered in the literature. (4) If you have been asked to discuss a statement, you will need to set out the conditions under which it holds

Heading	Subheadings and content
	('is true'), or the qualifications or limitations that you feel must be attached to it ('it depends').
CONCLUSIONS	(1) The briefest possible summary of your discussion. This is just to draw threads together, for the reader's benefit. Include the salient points only. You won't earn any marks for repeating yourself. (2) 'Revisit' your starting point. Summarize in one or two sentences your answer to the question set or the view you have formed on the statement you were asked to discuss.

Using quotations

When you find something in a piece of writing that attracts you and you want to quote from it, please think about what you want to use the quotation *for*, and how you can get the maximum benefit out of it. You will find it enormously helpful if you can get into the habit of asking what your quotation from a particular source actually contributes to your essay. Many student essays simply prefix a quotation with the words 'According to X, ...' or 'X states ...' and fail to make clear the *significance* of the quotation, leaving the reader wondering 'So what?' A good essay *does* make the significance of a quotation clear, and this has a three-fold payoff: in thinking about significance you develop your skill in reasoning and critical thinking; you demonstrate to the reader that you have put thought into the essay; and you are helping to insure yourself against the danger of plagiarism because the thoughts are your own.

The contribution made by a quotation may take one of a variety of forms: facts, perceptions, figures of speech (metaphors and similes), definitions, assumptions, propositions, opinions, value judgments, claims (e.g. in the form of appeals to common sense), questions and reasoning. Each kind of contribution (a) needs to be referred to in a particular way; and (b) invites you to ask certain questions about it. In Table 9 I go through the list of kinds of contribution: I suggest how you should refer to contributions of each kind in your text and offer some questions that you can ask about them.

Table 9: Using quotations

Type of contribution	How to refer to it	Questions to ask about it
Fact	X found, discovered, revealed, ascertained, notes, points out that	Is this fact universally accepted, accurate (so far as you can tell)? Have other significant facts been ignored? How am I using this fact?
Perception	X describes, identifies, distinguishes, categorizes; as X sees it, ...	Does X have a particular standpoint which causes him/her to perceive things in this particular way? Are there alternative standpoints?
Figure of speech	X regards ... as; compares ... to; suggests that ... is like ...	Is this an appropriate metaphor or simile? How does it assist my understanding? Do I want to adopt it?
Definition	X defines ... to mean ...	Do other writers have different definitions, i.e. attribute different meanings to the same term?
Assumption	X assumes, postulates, hypothesizes, conjectures, takes it for granted that	Do other writers make this assumption? Is it valid, justified? Do I wish to share it? If I make different assumptions, would I come to different conclusions?

Type of contribution	How to refer to it	Questions to ask about it
Proposition	X argues, asserts, contends, suggests, hypothesizes ... that if A, then B; X supports, is critical of, criticizes	How can I test the validity of this proposition, whether it 'fits the facts'?
Opinion	According to X; X tells us, says, thinks, suggests, considers, comments, agrees that; X disagrees with; in X's opinion; it seems to X that	On what grounds (evidence) does X base his opinions? Do other people hold them? If not, why not? Do I agree with X?
Value judgment	To X, it should, ought; to X it is good, bad, beneficial, harmful	Do other people share X's value judgments? Why should I pay attention to them?
Claim	X claims that in his/her professional judgment; to X, it surely, must be, is obvious that, is common sense that	What is the authority on which X bases his/her claim? Why shouldn't I challenge that claim and authority?
Question	X asks/questions whether	Are these questions relevant? Are there other questions that I ought to be asking?
Reasoning	X infers from this evidence that; shows from his/her analysis that; X demonstrates how; concludes	Is this reasoning sound? Could other conclusions be drawn from the same evidence?

The writing process

'Writing as thinking' and 'writing as assembly job'

Once you've produced a rough plan for your essay and done some targeted reading, you've already done quite a bit of thinking. Now you can begin to make a start on assembling. Collect your reading matter for the essay and spread it around you. Locate any notes that you've made, your annotated photocopies, and your books and articles bristling with Post-its. See which of them you can fit under the headings or subheadings in your essay plan. Revise your plan if necessary.

Another thing you can do is this. If you have some flip-chart paper stick your plan in the middle of a sheet and your Post-its and notes around it, and draw lines to show which of them are relevant to particular sections of your essay. Now stand back and look at the result. For some sections you may have more notes than you can use: think about which ones to select. (Yes, it can be very painful to discard material that you have worked hard on. Could you attach it to your essay as an appendix? Or might it come in handy when you're revising for exams?)

If for other sections you find yourself short of material, you have to plug or bridge the gap – or revise your plan again. From the scanning you did earlier, you may know which books or articles contain material that you could use for this purpose, and where exactly to find it. If not, identify the relevant key terms and scan for them to locate the material you need. When you come across it, take some time to think about its significance and how to use it.

Now it's time to get down to some serious writing: the assembly job. You can work on sections in any order. You may want to get some or all sections written in note form, and then polish the whole thing later. It's up to you: there is no one right way of doing it. But don't under any circumstances spend a lot of time on writing the perfect introduction before you can see where the essay as a whole is going.

A last word on thinking and assembling. For a really challenging essay, you may well find yourself doing a lot of writing as thinking. It isn't uncommon to find yourself already over your word limit with half the essay still to write, the deadline approaching, and a sense that the enterprise has got out of hand. You may have the feeling that it's 'diverging' – broadening out – rather than 'converging' – becoming focused. If this happens, stop what you're doing, stand back, and look at your structure, your 'framework' for assembly. Almost certainly you've parted company from the structure you started out with. There may be a number of signs that this is happening. You may have introduced new questions halfway through the essay, a sign that your methodology has changed as you have been thinking: promote them to your introduction. One of your sections (literature review, perhaps?) may be far too large: leave it for now but plan to edit it down when you've finished all the other sections. Your conclusions (if you have started drafting them) may not be an answer to the question set: review them immediately.

Getting a smooth 'flow'

You may be told that a well-written essay has a smooth 'flow': each paragraph or each section leads on smoothly and logically to the next. This isn't always easy to achieve. An essay has to be linear in form – each paragraph has only one before it and only one following it – whereas the thinking that you want to present may be in your head as a network of connected points.

Problems arise when you've spent a paragraph going into detail: in effect, you've gone down a branch line; how are you going to get back on to the main track? And when you've had to write something about each of several points or case studies 'in parallel', so to speak, how are you going to go smoothly forward after dealing with the last one?

The solution to these problems lies in making it crystal clear to the reader what you are doing. Provide a contents list for your essay, with subheadings and lists. Material under a subheading doesn't have to lead on to material under the next main heading: the reader won't expect it to, and won't be 'thrown' when it doesn't. And to get back on track after you've worked your way through several parallel points or case studies, it's a good idea to have a sentence or two drawing the separate strands together: by giving a summary or overview, for example.

Writing to a word limit (breadth versus depth)

If you have to write an essay that must not exceed a certain number of words, you may be faced with a dilemma. You don't know whether to deal with the topic broadly and not go into depth, or to deal with it narrowly but in depth: you can't do both. In effect, you have to make a trade-off between breadth and depth.

The problem is that taking the broad approach could lead you to write in generalities and broad generalizations, and lead to your essay being marked down as being too shallow, too superficial. Almost certainly your teacher will be looking for some depth in what you write. This could involve not so much providing detail but showing that you are aware of the subtleties of the subject – like finer variations, dependence on the particular circumstances of a situation, or possible errors or biases on the part of writers whom you've consulted – and/or showing that you have a grasp of the analytical methods required for an in-depth treatment.

Having said this, there is one sensible precaution to take. You need to show the reader that you are aware of the breadth of the subject and that you have made your selection of areas within the topic consciously – after some thought – rather than written about one or two areas because they're the only ones you know about.

So you might select three writers, or three case studies, because they illustrate two extremes and a mid-point. Having made your selection, you must be sure to tell your reader early in the essay what you have done, and why.

It probably hasn't escaped you that the 'breadth versus depth' dilemma applies on a wider scale to many (if not all) of the courses you are taking, especially if you are faced with monster reading lists. If you have accustomed yourself to combining an 'overview' approach with selective in-depth treatment of topics you will have gone a long way towards mastering the subject – and preparing yourself for exams too. But because teaching in higher education is such a personal matter, it would be prudent to find out whether your teachers disagree with any of this advice, and – if so – on what grounds.

Writing style

Don't write like a textbook! There's one feature of academics' writing and lecturing that you should not try to imitate: namely, the 'authority' with which they sometimes imbue their material. An academic may use authority-implying expressions such as 'We consider ...', 'In our judgment, ...', 'As so-and-so rightly says, ...'. All these expressions carry the implication that he or she is an authority on the subject and not to be challenged. If you as a student use them, what you say and write will strike your teachers as pretentious and inappropriate.

Some teachers have very definite views about style, and may mark your work down if they disapprove of yours. So before submitting an essay to anyone, or making a presentation in their presence, you should feel free to ask them any or all of the following questions:

- Is it acceptable for me to write in the first person, for example 'In this essay I shall show ...', 'I feel ...' and 'I conclude ...'? Or do you prefer impersonal forms, such as 'This essay will show ...', 'The present writer feels ...' and 'One would conclude ...'?

- Do you prefer essays to be written in the active voice (e.g. 'Germany invaded Poland') rather than the passive voice (e.g. 'Poland was invaded by Germany')?

- Is it acceptable to use headings and subheadings in my essays? Some teachers feel that these interfere with the 'flow' of the prose. It could well be that 'main' headings will be acceptable but subheadings will not.

- Is it acceptable to make use of case studies or other materials that weren't on the reading list but I found for myself?

- Will I be penalized for spelling mistakes in essays or for using the American spellings for words?

- Will I be penalized if I express views that disagree with yours?

I offer you these suggestions as a matter of practical politics, in recognition of the fact that as a student you are situated at a low level in a power structure, and that it is a power structure in which language is used to claim and assert authority. Have you encountered that expression beloved of academics 'The evidence suggests ...'? Evidence on its own suggests nothing whatever, of course. The accurate expression would be 'On the basis of this evidence I think that ...' But in the culture of UK higher education to use such language would amount to an abdication of authority.

In the interests of user-friendliness, I have written this book using the informal language of spoken English as much as possible – expressions such as 'bits' and 'a lot', for example. There are two dangers that you may encounter if you do this in academic writing: it may lead you to be imprecise, and it may give the impression that you are sloppy and non-rigorous – even journalistic (a term of abuse in some academic circles) – in the way that you think.

I suggest, therefore, that you avoid the following words and expressions (possible alternatives are given in brackets):

- 'it's' (it is) (avoid *all* such contractions)
- 'bits' (parts)
- 'things' (units, elements, factors)
- 'a lot' or 'a load' (a significant amount, a sizeable quantity, considerable numbers)
- 'like' (similar to, such as)

- 'get' (obtain, receive, become)
- 'as well as' (in addition to)
- 'How come ...?' (What caused, what brought about ...?)

The rule is: avoid 'chatty', conversational language!

Part Five

Referencing styles

Using and citing sources

Using other people's writings as sources and acknowledging their contribution by 'citing' the source – i.e. supplying a reference to it – is central to academic writing. Citing your sources is not only a way of providing you with an important protection against being accused of plagiarism: it is also good academic practice. It shows a proper concern on your part with the quality of the evidence you have used and with substantiating your conclusion. In any worthwhile essay that you write, your reasoning will involve making use of what others before you have written. Citing your sources will enable the reader to check that you have used those sources appropriately and that your reasoning is sound. This is the intellectual – as opposed to the self-protective – justification for citing your sources. Using and citing sources involves providing three things:

- an extract from the source (a word-for-word quotation or your own paraphrase of a quotation) or a statement of your own to which the source is relevant;
- an insert of some kind in the text: a cue, marker or 'signpost' that directs the reader to a place where details of the source can be found;
- a listing of the details of your sources.

Incorporating extracts into your text

Short extracts: If you are quoting directly (rather than paraphrasing), and the extract is not more than a certain length – this could be two lines, three lines, 30 words or 40 words: check with whatever referencing style guide you're using (see below) – enclose it in quotation marks. Check with your style guide too to see whether these should be single or double quotation marks. If the extract already includes a word, phrase or sentence in quotation marks, the guide may tell you that these should be double if the 'outside' ones are single, and vice versa.

Longer extracts: If your extract is longer than two or three lines, indent it. Your style guide may tell you whether it should be indented from both margins or only the left-hand one. An indented extract should not be enclosed in quotation marks.

Shortened extracts: It is permissible to shorten an extract by taking out words, as long as you do not change the author's meaning. (Never remove the word 'not', for example!) The fact that words have been taken out is shown by the insertion of (usually) three dots (i.e. full stops, or periods). Your own words can be inserted in place of the author's: this is usually done so that the extract still reads grammatically. Your own words should be enclosed in square brackets and again you must not change the author's meaning. If, as a result of your shortening, a word that was formerly inside a sentence now begins one, the first letter of that word may be enclosed in square brackets. (Again, consult your style guide: it may or may not require this.)

Paraphrasing: If you are paraphrasing someone else's work, it is important to make it clear that you are doing so: use some formula like 'to paraphrase X, …'; 'X appears to be assuming/arguing/suggesting …'; 'in other words …' (after an actual quotation).

The bewildering variety of referencing styles

Please note that there is no single right way of referencing. Ask your teachers if they have preferences as to which referencing style you should use, *and* either to supply you with a style guide or to refer you to one. In some fields (medicine, law) there are standard styles in the UK and USA and other English-speaking countries, but in others there are not. Some publishers and journals have their own distinctive house style, too. As a second best, ask your teachers to suggest a book or a journal whose style you can follow.

There are, as far as I can see, four kinds of referencing style in general use. You can easily tell which is being used in a book or article that you're reading because they have different kinds of citation, i.e. insert in the text. Look out for the following:

- Author and date, e.g. Smith (1980) or (Smith, 1980). Full details of Smith's 1980 publication are contained in a list at the end of the book, the chapter or the article. I refer to this as the **author/date** style.

- Author and page number, e.g. Jones (117) or (Jones 117). I refer to this as the **author/page** style.

- Superscript, e.g. [12] The superscript, or raised number, directs you to a footnote (at the foot of the page) or endnote (at the end of the book, chapter or article) with the same number. Full details of the publication are contained in the footnote or endnote. I refer to this as the **numbered-note** style. (The British Standards Institution publication *BS 5605:1990, Recommendations for citing and referencing published material* (BSI 1990), describes it as the 'running notes' method.) It is the style used in this book.

- Bracketed numbers, e.g. (12). Like the numbered-note style, the bracketed number directs you to a footnote (at the foot of the page) or endnote (at the end of the book, chapter or article) with the same number. The best-known version of this is the Vancouver style, but you'll also find it referred to as the 'numeric' style, so I refer to it as the **Vancouver-numeric** style. Unlike the numbered-note style, the same number (bracketed) may appear in more than one place in the text.

Which style to choose?

If you have an essay to write, and you have some choice when it comes to selecting a referencing style, which one should you choose? Here are some things you should know about the four main kinds:

The author/date style

Varieties: In the UK and Australia the most common version of the author/date style is that known as the Harvard style. In the USA the APA, ASA/ASR and CBE and AIP styles are versions of this style. It is commonly used in the physical and life sciences and the social sciences.[1]

Inserts in the text: In the text you place an insert giving the author(s) and date of publication. For example: 'Smith (1980) describes X as ...' or 'X has been described (Smith, 1980) as ...'.

If Smith had two publications in 1980, they are differentiated by putting letters (a, b ...) after the year. So if you are referring to both at different places, your text with inserts would look something like: 'Smith (1980a) describes ...' and 'Smith (1980b) concludes ...'. You might also want or be required to include page numbers, so that the reader does not have to wade through Smith's book in its entirety to find your source. Then your text with inserts would look something like: 'Smith (1980a, p.13) describes ...' or 'Some writers have concluded (e.g. Smith, 1980b: 17–18) ...'. Your style guide should tell you whether or not you are required to prefix page numbers by p. or pp., and whether it should be '(Smith, 1980)' or '(Smith 1980)'.

Listing: For every different insert, you write a reference saying where the source can be found. At the end of your essay you attach a list of all the references, in alphabetical order of authors' surnames. This list might be headed 'Bibliography', 'List of references', or 'Works cited'. There are a number of ways in which entries in the list could be set out – different style guides prescribe different ones – but they all have in common that they begin something like: 'Smith, T. (1980) ...'.

Usefulness: The author/date style is most useful where all your sources are books or journal articles with one or more designated authors. The insertion of dates in the text may be helpful, as Ritter points out, for following the progress of a debate.[2] This style also allows you to add or subtract references easily if you have occasion to amend your essay just before handing it in. It is less useful if you have to deal with 'messy' sources like newspaper articles and editorials, the publications of government bodies or other organizations where no author is credited, broadcasts on TV or radio, or websites. And it is of no use as a vehicle for 'parenthetical' comments – asides – that you don't want to place in the body of your essay.

The author/page style

Varieties: The main (if not the only) version of this style is the MLA style, codified by the Modern Language Association in the USA.

Inserts in the text: In the text you place an insert giving the author(s) and the number of the page. For example: 'Jones (117) describes X as ...' or 'X has been described (Jones 117) as ...'. If you are referring to two different publications both authored by Jones, they are differentiated by including the title, which may be abbreviated.

Listing: At the end of your essay you attach a list of all the sources you have cited, in alphabetical order of authors' surnames. This list should be headed 'Works cited'.

Usefulness: The author/page style is most useful where all your sources are books or journal articles with one or more designated authors. If your source is an article in a bulky newspaper, citing the page is good practice since it will help the reader to track down the article. It can also work satisfactorily even if no author is credited, because you can cite the title instead. It is less good with websites and, like the author-date style, is of no use as a vehicle for 'parenthetical' comments – asides – that you don't want to place in the body of your essay.

The numbered-note style

Varieties: Numbered-note styles include the Chicago and Turabian styles well known in the USA. In Australia, the so-called Oxford style and Cambridge style are also of this kind. In the UK, you may find it referred to as the traditional footnote style or the endnote style, or – as by the British Standards Institution – the 'running notes' style. It is commonly used in the arts and humanities, some social and political science fields, and law.

Inserts in the text: At every point where you wish to supply a reference or a comment of some kind, you insert a superscript, a raised number. You start with [1], then [2], and so on, through the essay. Even if you are referring to a source that you have already referred to, you give it a new number. (So no superscript number appears twice.) Variants of this style place the footnote number in round or square brackets. Footnote numbers should follow, not precede full stops.

Listing: For every superscript, you write a note giving the reference and/or making your comment. These notes may be placed at the foot of the page on which the superscript appears, in which case they are footnotes, or they may be placed at the end of the essay, in which case they are endnotes. The notes will be listed in numerical order to correspond with the superscripts. The list of endnotes can appropriately be headed 'Notes and references'.

In addition to the list of notes and references, you may be asked by your teachers to provide a bibliography. Normally this would be a list of books and articles that you have used for 'background' reading: ask whether works listed in your notes should also be listed in your bibliography.

Usefulness: The great thing about the numbered-note style is that you can use it not only for references but for those parenthetical comments and asides that would interrupt the flow if you put them in the body of your text: a comment on the reliability of a source, or on some quirk that it exhibits; a reminder to the reader what certain abbreviations stand for; a signpost to another source where a different point of view can be found; and so on. It is also convenient to use when you are citing an original source which a 'secondary' source led you to: you can simply cite the original and then say 'cited by' the secondary source.

The numbered-note style can be cumbersome if you've inserted all your superscripts and then decide you want to add or subtract a reference, because this entails renumbering all the subsequent references. One way of getting round this is by using your word processor's automatic footnote/ endnote system: another way – which I use – is to type out each note within your text and enclose it within ## ... ##: when you've finalized the text you can find these one by one, remove each one from the text on to the clipboard and substitute the relevant superscript, and then copy them from the clipboard in batches of ten into your 'Notes and references' list.

The Vancouver-numeric style

Varieties: The Vancouver style emerged from a meeting of editors of general medical journals in Vancouver, Canada, in 1978 to establish guidelines for the format of manuscripts submitted to their journals. The group agreed a set of guidelines which was first published in 1979 and defines the Vancouver style. The latest version, *Uniform Requirements for Manuscripts Submitted to Biomedical Journals*, is effectively the norm for biomedical journals. The numeric system described very briefly in *BS 5605:1990* is very similar.

Inserts in the text: At every point where you wish to supply a reference to a source you have used, you insert a number in brackets (parentheses). (*BS 5605:1990* offers the choice of using superscripts instead.) Similarly to numbered notes, you start with (1), then (2), and so on, through the essay. *But* when you refer to a source that you have previously referred to, you insert its *original* number (unlike the numbered-note style). So if you refer to source no. 3 seven times, say, the insert (3) will appear seven times in your text.

Listing: For every insert, you write a reference saying where the source can be found. Your list of references will go at the end of your essay, in numerical order to correspond with the inserts. The list can appropriately be headed 'References'.

Usefulness: Like the author/date style, the Vancouver-numeric style is most useful where all your sources are books or journal articles with one or more designated authors. The inserts are less distracting than authors, dates and page numbers. But if you have referred to different parts of the book in different places in your text it does not offer you an elegant method of citing the different page numbers in a book: it is therefore most effective where your sources are relatively compact, like journal articles or self-contained chapters in a book.

The Vancouver-numeric style is more economical than the numbered-note style in that only one reference is needed for each source (and so you will have no occasion to use *ibid.*, *op. cit.* or *loc. cit.*). But it is less useful if you have to deal with 'messy' sources, and it is of no use as a vehicle for parenthetical comments.

Listing and detailing your sources

If you are using the author-date (e.g. Harvard) or author-page style, your list will be arranged in alphabetical order of author's (or first author's) surnames. For a single-author book, the layout will usually be as follows:

Author's surname | Author's initials or first name | Year of publication | Title (usually in italics but may be underlined) | Number of edition if not the first | Place of publication (followed by a colon) | Publisher

If you are using the Vancouver-numeric style, your list will be arranged in the numerical order of your bracketed inserts. For a single-author book, the layout will be as follows:

Author's surname | Author's initials or first name (but these can go before the surname if preferred) | Title (usually in italics but may be underlined) | Number of edition if not the first | Place of publication (followed by a colon) | Publisher | Year of publication

As you can see, the main difference from the Harvard style is that the date of publication is placed at the end of the reference rather than directly after the author's name.

If you are using the numbered-note style, your list will be arranged in the numerical order of your superscripts. This style does offer you some choice in laying out your references. For a single-author book, here are three possibilities:

Author's surname | Author's initials or first name | Title | Number of edition if not the first | Place of publication (followed by a colon) | Publisher | Year of publication | Page number(s)

Author's initials or first name | Author's surname | Title | Number of edition if not the first | Place of publication (followed by a colon) | Publisher | Year of publication | Page number(s)

Author's initials or first name | Author's surname | Year of publication (in brackets) | Title | Number of edition if not the first | Page number(s) | Place of publication (followed by a colon) | Publisher

If you are using the numbered-note style, you may find yourself referring to the same source a number of times. There are conventions that you can use to save yourself copying out the reference afresh each time: the '*ibid.*', '*op. cit.*' and '*loc. cit.*' conventions. *Ibid.* is an abbreviation of *ibidem*, a Latin word meaning 'in the same place'. *Op. cit.* is an abbreviation of *opere citato*, a Latin phrase meaning 'in the work cited'. *Loc. cit.* is an abbreviation of *loco citato*, Latin for 'in the place cited'. (As you can see, I'm adopting the convention here of putting words that are in a foreign language in italics.) You can use *ibid.* when a note refers to the same source as does the previous note, either the same page or a different one. You can use *op. cit.* to refer to a work previously cited in the same list. And you can use *loc. cit.* when you are referring to the same place in a work previously cited in the same list. For example:

18 P. Levin (1997) *Making Social Policy*, p. 30. Buckingham: Open University Press.

19 *Ibid.*, p. 65 [Same author and book as in previous note but different page]

20 *Ibid.* [Same author, same book and same page as in previous note]

21 J.G. March and H.A. Simon (1958) *Organizations*, pp. 140–1. New York: Wiley.

22 Levin, *op. cit.*, p. 222. [The work by Levin previously cited in this list, but a different page]

23 March and Simon, *loc. cit.* [The work by March and Simon previously cited in this list, and the same page]

If the use of Latin strikes you as too archaic for words, you can do something like this:

18 P. Levin (1997) *Making Social Policy*, p. 30. Buckingham: Open University Press.

19 Levin, note 18, p. 65 [Same author and book as in previous note but different page]

20 As note 19 [Same author, same book and same page as in previous note]

21 J.G. March and H.A. Simon (1958) *Organizations*, pp. 140–1. New York: Wiley.

22 Levin, note 18, p. 222. [The work by Levin previously cited in this list, but a different page]

23 As note 21 [The work by March and Simon previously cited in this list, and the same page]

There are actually British Standards that give recommendations for citing and referencing published materials,[3] and these can be applied to whichever style you're using, so they're available if you haven't been given any specific instructions about style.

Best websites for referencing styles

At the time of going to press, the following websites were offering useful material on referencing styles:

Author/date style

http://www.lmu.ac.uk/lss/ls/docs/harvfron.htm [Accessed 21 June 2004] Dee, M., Leeds Metropolitan University (1998) *Quote, Unquote: The Harvard Style of Referencing Published Material.*

http://owl.english.purdue.edu/handouts/research/r_apa.html [Accessed 21 June 2004] Purdue University Online Writing Lab (OWL) (2001) *Using American Psychological Association (APA) Format.*

Author/page style

http://owl.english.purdue.edu/handouts/research/r_mla.html [Accessed 21 June 2004] Purdue University Online Writing Lab (OWL) (2000) *Using Modern Language Association (MLA) Format.*

Numbered-note style

http://www.deakin.edu.au/learningservices/pub_manual/oxford_ref.php [Accessed 21 June 2004] Learning Services, Deakin University (2001) *Oxford Referencing Style.*

Vancouver-numeric style

http://www.icmje.org/ [Accessed 21 June 2004] International Committee of Medical Journal Editors (2003) *Uniform Requirements for Manuscripts Submitted to Biomedical Journals.*

Recording details of your sources

Citing sources will be easier to do if you make a habit of recording their details at the time when you take notes from them. When you're photocopying pages from a book save yourself some work by photocopying the title page too, because it will have some of the details you need (don't forget to add the year of publication to your photocopied title page).

For a 'unitary' book (i.e. written as a whole, not a compilation of chapters by different authors), record the following:

- The name(s) of the author(s)
- The title and subtitle
- The year of publication
- The edition, if not the first

- The publisher
- The city or town where the publisher's main office is situated
- The number(s) of the relevant pages.

  For a chapter in a 'compilation' book:

- The name(s) of the author(s) of the chapter
- The title of the chapter
- The title and subtitle of the book
- The name(s) of the editor(s) of the book
- The year of publication
- The publisher
- The city or town where the publisher's main office is situated
- The number(s) of the relevant pages.

  For an article in a journal:

- The name(s) of the author(s)
- The title of the article
- The title of the journal and any standard abbreviation of the title
- The year of publication
- The number of the volume of the journal
- The part number of the journal and month/season of publication
- The number(s) of the relevant pages.

  For an item on a web page:

- The URL (uniform resource locator) of the page, otherwise known as its web address
- The date on which you accessed the page.

It is sensible to copy and paste the URL into a document to guard against errors in copying by hand, especially if the URL is one of those monster database-generated ones whose rhyme and reason are known only to the webmaster.

And

Be sure to store the web page electronically, and also to print it out, so you have it to refer to if the page is subsequently altered or becomes unavailable. And watch out for line breaks (*never* insert a hyphen, as this will change the URL) and for underscores concealed by an underline.

Finally

Whichever referencing style you use for your essays, try to be 100 per cent accurate, complete and consistent in your referencing. In particular, pay attention to spelling authors' names correctly. A spellchecker won't help you with these, and errors in spelling names will give a poor impression to the reader.

It may be that your teacher will want you to list not only the sources on which you have drawn for particular material but also your background reading on the subject. Normally this will require only a separate list – 'Background reading' – but if you are using the Harvard system your teacher might prefer you to include those items in your main list.

Part Six

Plagiarism and collusion

The conscientious student's predicament

'Plagiarism' is a subject on which some academics these days are exceedingly twitchy. They report more and more cases of students submitting written work that in whole or in part appears to have been composed by other people, without citing its source.[1] In some cases this is undoubtedly cheating (in the sense of acting with intention to deceive), as when large amounts of material have been 'lifted' – taken verbatim – from an unacknowledged source, or systematic efforts have been made to conceal the fact that other people's material has been used (e.g. attributing only some of the 'borrowed' material, changing the order of items in a list, making minor alterations in wording).

Understandably, cheating is taken particularly seriously when the mark for the work submitted will count towards students' degree results, because if it is not detected they may be awarded a better result than they have earned. And this, of course, is seen as detrimental to the public standing of the institution's degrees, as well as grossly unfair to all the conscientious, law-abiding students who have worked hard for their results.

Universities have reacted to this situation in a predictable and often cack-handed manner, by producing their own definitions of 'plagiarism' and accompanying regulations, and issuing stern warnings couched in highly emotive language: plagiarism is 'cheating', 'theft', 'stealing', 'dishonest', 'a crime'. In some places a threatening, intimidating atmosphere has been created. New students may have to sign plagiarism statements immediately on arrival saying they're aware of the seriousness of plagiarism and the penalties it incurs. So you turn up at uni, stand in a queue to register, are told 'sign here', and given no time to read the small print. In effect, you are welcomed to the academic community with a message from their teachers saying: 'We regard you as potentially dishonest, a cheat and a thief, and we are watching you!'

And the regulations and warnings are often highly confusing. There tends to be a common core – you mustn't pass off other people's work as your own, which is fair enough – but they all give rise to more questions. If you unintentionally don't cite a source, does that count as plagiarism? If you use two or three phrases that you dimly recollect from a lecture or some article you've read, without attributing them, does that make you guilty of plagiarism? How close to an unattributed original does paraphrasing have to be for it to be plagiarism? And what counts as 'common knowledge', so you don't need to reference it?

But the word 'plagiarism' is interpreted by different people to mean different things, and different academics would give different answers to these questions. Many would regard unintentional failure to cite a source, or failure to attribute a dimly-recollected phrase or two, or paraphrasing of an unattributed original into which some work has evidently been put, or an error of judgment as to what can be treated as common knowledge, as poor academic practice rather than outright cheating.

You may be further confused if your teachers insist that your work must be 'original', 'unaided', or not 'derived from somewhere else'.[2] This is another minefield! In fact, even a University of London MPhil thesis doesn't require to be original, as long as it is 'an ordered and critical exposition of existing knowledge and [provides] evidence that the field has been surveyed thoroughly'.[3] Logically, then, originality shouldn't be a necessary condition for gaining a Bachelor's degree either. And I would respectfully suggest that the whole point of going to university and pursuing a degree course is that you *are* aided in your work, and that you *do* learn how to 'derive' your opinions and conclusions from the work of others, given that – as noted above – the focus of academic learning is the views of other people.

All in all, the current confusion surrounding plagiarism and originality creates a predicament for conscientious, hard-working, law-abiding students, and some have certainly been penalized for unwittingly breaking the university's rules on plagiarism, despite having no intention to cheat. In the following sections I offer some suggestions for conscientious students for avoiding accusations of plagiarism, and defending yourself if you do find you're accused.

How academic learning forces you to plagiarize

One of the dictionary definitions of 'plagiarism' is 'appropriating [the thoughts, writings, etc.] of others'. In this sense, plagiarism is actually integral to the Western system of propagating knowledge and ideas through higher education, because – to repeat Diana Laurillard's words once more – 'it is a peculiarity of academic learning that its focus is not the world itself but others' views of that world'.[1] The great majority of what you are required to learn is based on the documented views – the perceptions and thoughts – of others, not on your own experience. You read and listen, you copy out, you make your notes, you paraphrase (that's to say, you translate academic-speak into language you can understand), and you absorb, you digest, *other people's work*. It's 'honest plagiarism', if you like. Far from being 'cheating', appropriating from others is central to academic learning.

Getting a solid grounding in a subject must necessarily entail absorbing other people's views, internalizing them. Do this successfully and you won't know – you *can't* know – where your views begin and someone else's end. In much the same way as children are brought up by their parents and in the process take on unconsciously their attitudes, their ways of being and thinking and looking at the world, and of course their language, successful students find themselves being brought up by their teachers and undergo an analogous 'bringing-up' process in the course of becoming a historian or physicist or whatever, similarly picking up attitudes, ways of being and thinking, and – crucially – ideas and language: expressions, turns of phrase, ways of describing, explaining, arguing. Without the solid grounding created by such a process, you won't have a firm base on which to develop and build views of your own.

In 'Three stages in academic learning', pages 12–14, I suggested that academic learning proceeds in three repeating stages: (1) selecting and copying, as in making notes; (2) translating, as in paraphrasing and annotating; and (3) digesting: 'engaging' with the subject, thinking and reasoning in the subject's language.

Selecting and copying

When you first take notes, the words are of course those of the author: they still 'belong' to that person. But the notes are *your* notes, and as you become familiar with them you appropriate them: you 'internalize' them, you incorporate them into your personal knowledge and understanding of the subject. So what you are doing, it seems to me, is performing a kind of private plagiarism. You are – *of necessity* – appropriating other people's material. And the more effectively that you do this, the more difficult it is to attribute sources.

If you are being pushed to write an essay on a topic that is new to you, and so are at the 'selecting and copying' stage, you could probably use the notes you have taken to cobble something together, assembling a string of quotations and taking care to cite your source for each. If your quotations are relevant and presented in a logical order, they will show that you have done some reading and/or taken some notes in lectures, that you have an ability to distinguish the relevant from the not-relevant, and that you possess an appropriate concept of how an essay should be structured.

In my personal judgment, marking criteria *should* include evidence of reading, of a sense of relevance, and of a grasp of structure: an essay that demonstrates these qualities has some merit. However, I may be a lone voice here: nothing that I have read on the subject of plagiarism suggests that others share my view. It is possible that your own teachers would share it: you will need to ask. *But* essay topics and exam questions should be – which does not mean to say that they actually are – designed to see if you have progressed beyond that level, and in that case your teacher clearly would not be satisfied with such an essay. (If the topic is framed as a question, it is quite probable that you would not be answering it.)

Translating

Translating involves expressing the words that you read or hear into different words, so you produce an 'equivalent' statement that, all being well, makes sense to you. That is to say, it involves you in *paraphrasing* the original statement. You can see from various definitions of 'plagiarism' that paraphrasing carries the same dangers of plagiarizing as direct quoting does. Again, as with quotations, you are – of necessity – appropriating your paraphrasings as your own: you are 'internalizing' them, incorporating them into your personal understanding and conceptions of the subject matter. So translating too positively *forces* you to plagiarize, if only to yourself.

If you are still at the 'translating' stage on the topic, your essay is likely to be made up of very simply paraphrased quotations: word-for-word substitution – probably involving you in looking up many words in an appropriate dictionary or textbook – while keeping the same sentence structure. Your teacher will be looking for you to cite the original sources: if you don't do so, it will look as though you are trying to pass off the material as your own, and you could be accused of plagiarism. As with direct quotations, if your paraphrasings are relevant and presented in a logical order, they will show that you have 'taken on board' some material and have some sense of relevance and structure: in addition, the essay will show that you have begun to make progress in 'digesting' the material.

Would your teacher be satisfied with *this*? Again, you will need to ask. *But*, if the essay topic is designed to test your ability to reason (i.e. the main marking criterion is: Does this essay provide evidence of ability to reason?) your teacher clearly would not be satisfied. And again, if the topic is framed as a question, you would quite probably not be answering it.

Digesting

When you break through from selecting/copying and translating to digesting a subject, you're still in some danger of involuntary plagiarizing. When you're fluent in a subject, you're thinking in its language unconsciously. To me, an appropriate analogy to this process is that of learning to dance. For some people, this involves first getting the moves into your head, then getting them into your feet, then getting them out of your head. At this point you're dancing without consciously thinking about it. For academics to demand of students who are fluent in a subject that they cite in a piece of written work every source that they've drawn on is like insisting that they learn to dance with their shoes tied together.

It's not only students who encounter this difficulty. You may be interested to see a 43-page report prepared in May 2001 for the Joint Information Systems Committee: *Plagiarism: A Good Practice Guide.* (Don't be confused by its title: this is *not* a guide to making a good job of plagiarizing.) Its authors, Jude Carroll and Jon Appleton, acknowledge that their suggestions and recommendations arise from a range of sources, not all of which they have cited:

> Some ... are gleaned from the experience of colleagues or more experienced practitioners, from conversations with a wide range of people at conferences, and from consultations with student representatives ... Where appropriate, sources and research findings are cited but it has not always been possible to unearth the exact origin of ideas or to use publicly available sources.[2]

The fact that experts in detecting plagiarism don't always find it possible to unearth the exact origin of ideas they have used sits oddly with the frequently encountered injunction to students that *they* must do so. And I think it corroborates my suggestion that taking in other people's ideas is something that can happen at a subconscious level, and that the nature of academic learning, where you are required to absorb the work of others, is such that it positively *forces* you to begin by plagiarizing, if only to yourself.

If plagiarism is so deeply engrained in the academic culture, how can you avoid laying yourself open to being accused of it? In the next section I offer some suggestions as to what you can do.

Avoiding accusations of plagiarism

The prime way of avoiding accusations of plagiarism is to develop good academic practice. In a sense, the whole of this book has been about developing good academic practice. From coping with monster reading lists, via exploratory, dedicated and targeted reading, to discovering what's wanted from you in your essays, clarifying your topic, thinking through your methodology, planning your essay, using quotations appropriately, assembling your essay and referencing it properly, my emphasis has been not only on doing the job but on doing it in a way that embodies high academic standards.

Here are some final points.

Question what you read

Get into the habit of questioning everything that you read. Ask yourself: 'Where does the writer get this from? How does he or she know? What assumptions or value judgments are being made here? How can I test that theory or model?' Check your answers with your teacher, at least while you're still gaining your confidence. This is a very good way of getting into the mindset of writers and developing the skill of reading critically.

There is an important point here for Master's students who have done their first degree at a different university, especially one outside the UK. You may previously have been in an educational system where you were expected to be able to quote authorities and textbooks, and were rewarded for doing no more than this. At your present university it may not be the same. You are likely to find that you are expected to *use* quotations to answer the question set for you. In other words, you have to digest the quotations you want to use – not merely reproduce them – and show in your essay that you have understood their relevance to the topic.

Collusion: take care when working with other students!

You may find that you are warned not only against committing plagiarism but also against committing 'collusion', conspiring with one or more other students to improve your marks by working together. Of course, students have always worked together – these may be among your most memorable and valuable learning experiences – and today we have the bizarre situation in many UK universities that on the one hand they are actually encouraging students to develop their teamwork skills, yet on the other hand they are warning them against collusion!

How should you respond to these mixed messages? I would certainly encourage you to work with other students: you will learn from them as well as from your teachers, and you will usually be able to express ideas and ask questions without feeling that you are being judged, which may not be the case in 'official' tutorials, classes and seminars. And you may find essays written by other students easier to learn from than texts written by academics, because they are written by people who are at a similar stage of the learning process to yourself. Indeed, you may find them mercifully free from the academic-speak and pontificating to which many academics are sadly prone. But do stop short of drafting essays or parts of essays together. The final selection of words must emerge from your own mind: it must be your own. Otherwise the sniffers-out of plagiarism will be on your tracks.

Don't throw away your notes

The notes that you make while working on an essay are evidence that the essay is your own work. You may be asked to produce them if a question of plagiarism or collusion arises. So keep them: on no account throw them away or destroy them when you've finished the essay.

Claim copyright for your own work

It is not unknown for academics to get ideas from their students and pass them off as their own. If an essay is genuinely your own work, and you have properly acknowledged material drawn from other sources, you are morally entitled to claim copyright for it. Indeed, if you have truthfully signed some kind of declaration that it is your own work, it follows that copyright belongs to you. To claim copyright, all you need do is add © Your Name 2004 (or whatever the year is) at the foot of the title page or at the end of the document. (In Micrososft Word, for © type [Ctrl] + [Alt] + [C].)

Resist temptation

If you are one of a large cohort of students taking a course, it may sometimes feel as though having to supply essays at regular intervals is exactly like having to satisfy a dog by providing it with regular meals. The temptation is to do the equivalent of going to the supermarket, purchasing a tin of dog food, opening it and spooning it into a bowl. Beware! Academics want home-prepared food, and they are going to judge you on it, which is why they are so antagonistic to your passing off shop-bought food as home-made. Even if you are using bought-in, ready-to-use ingredients, you must add something of your own – an additional ingredient or two, for example, or a variation on the method of preparation, cooking or presentation. Do your own little research project: try to work out what it is that will give your offerings 'teacher appeal'. But note that teachers, like dogs, are not all alike: subtle variations may be necessary to appeal to different academic tastes.

To plagiarize and successfully conceal the fact takes hard work. You may as well devote that work to doing the job properly. Don't be tempted, even if you are up against a deadline, to buy an essay from an outfit advertising on the web and submit it as your own work. This really is asking for trouble. Doing this raises no subtle questions of what is meant by 'plagiarism': it is an absolutely clear-cut case of cheating. The existence of highly developed plagiarism-detection software today makes it almost certain that you will be found out. You will be severely penalized – possibly being refused a degree or expelled from the institution – and subjected to a great deal of public humiliation, involving being branded as dishonest and a cheat. So I definitely do not recommend this course of action. Even if you submit a hand-written essay, it is almost impossible to avoid giving clues if you have used someone else's material word-for-word or in a close paraphrasing. Most academics love detective work, especially if they can feel righteous about it, and you are challenging them in their specialist field. Don't even try!

I would just add that in my experience students who actively try to master the language of their subjects, who question what they read, who read more than one book on a topic and check out original sources, and who actively seek feedback from their teachers and discuss their subjects with other students, tend to be the ones who get good results. Try to be one of them, and passing off other people's work as your own is the last thing you'll need to do in order to get good marks.

The politics of plagiarism

Check out your institution's rules and regulations

It will pay you to become familiar with your institution's rule-book, code of practice, or whatever, on the subject of 'plagiarism'. This will help you to keep out of trouble, and to keep a level head if there are rumours flying around about what does and does not count as 'plagiarism'. And if you get on the wrong side of any of your teachers, knowing the rules and complying with them will help you to avoid giving someone an excuse to accuse you of breaking them.

Notice how the rules are constituted. The more lengthy and detailed they are, and the more attention they give to spelling out offences rather than offering help, the more likely it is that those who drew them up are afflicted by paranoia on the subject. There may not be

117

much that you can do about that, but you should at least be aware of it.

Keep an eye open too for inconsistencies in the rules. They provide evidence of the confusion that exists among academics. A policy riddled with inconsistencies and rooted in confusion is always open to challenge. Look out too for words and phrases that require those who enforce rules to make judgments in interpreting them: 'substantial', 'extensive use' etc. Such judgments too may well be open to challenge.

Finally, if you are expected to cite your sources in a particular style – it will usually be the Harvard style or the numbered-note style – make sure you know what you're doing. If you're given a style guide, follow it. If you aren't supplied with one, ask where you can get one.

Check out your institution's practices

Rules and regulations are one thing: how they are enforced in practice may be quite another. Someone in your student union should have the job of keeping track of hearings into cases of alleged plagiarism, and reading reports on cases, paying particular attention to the evidence and criteria on which decisions were taken. He or she should be able to tell whether the institution is primarily concerned to prevent cheating or to enforce every minute detail of its plagiarism code and inflict the full force of the disciplinary machinery even on small-scale, inadvertent transgressions.

Note how much discretion academics have. It may be a matter for their judgment (a) whether the evidence supports the allegation that plagiarism has taken place; (b) if it does, whether it is a mild or severe offence; (c) whether there are extenuating circumstances; and (d) what the penalty should be. Different people may make different judgments (academics disagree with one another) and the membership of committees changes from year to year. Whether a student appears at a hearing or not, and is represented or not, may also influence the judgments that are made. However, a student accused of plagiarism is entitled to expect that his or her treatment will be consistent with previous cases, and if your institution shows what appears to be an undue concern with 'petty' plagiarism it will be worth examining the records of past cases to see whether they have been treated consistently: have similar cases incurred similar penalties?

It would also be worth inspecting cases to see whether students have been penalized for what is really poor academic practice rather than plagiarism. The line between these may well be blurred, in which case where it is drawn in a particular case may well be open to challenge.

Finally, you may also be able to challenge decisions if the regulations are imprecise, or it has not been made clear to you how they would apply in common situations: if, for example, you have not been told whether, if you have an idea that you think is your very own, you will be penalized or not if it turns out later that it's in someone's book. Or if you have not been told how to judge whether something can be taken as common knowledge, and therefore does not need to be referenced.

Box 4

Get some useful feedback

It is a common complaint among students that they don't get useful feedback on their essays. Sometimes the complaint is that marks aren't given, so they don't know how they are doing; sometimes it's that comments are very sketchy or that they are all criticism, and don't help the student to do better next time.

How essays should be marked is actually quite a tricky question, and I can understand why some teachers duck it. For example, if your course is one that 'builds' through the year rather than being divided into self-contained chunks, your teachers may well have a problem in deciding what is an appropriate basis for assessment. Should they mark an essay written midway through a course as they would if it had been written at the end of the year? That would be unduly tough, I think, and you might well find a mark awarded on this basis very discouraging. Should they mark an essay in the light of the fact that you wrote it only a few weeks into the course? The mark awarded would probably give you a false sense of your level and the standards expected overall, and if it led you to rely on the essay for revision for your exam you might do rather poorly.

Rather than press your teacher for a mark, I suggest you ask the four crucial feedback questions:

- What did I do well?
- What did I not do well?
- How could I have improved the essay?
- How can I do better next time?

Considered answers to these questions will help you to see what progress you are making, and will be of far more value to you than a mark.

Box 5

Web links, feedback, updates

Links to useful websites can be found by logging on to

www.student-friendly-guides.com

If you have any questions about reading and essay writing that this book hasn't covered, or any suggestions for improving it, please log on to the website and email them to me. I'll be glad to answer any questions, and all suggestions for improvements will be very gratefully received.

And don't forget to check out the website regularly for updates to this and other student-friendly guides.

Notes and references

The strange world of the university. READ THIS FIRST!

1   Diana Laurillard, *Rethinking University Education* (Routledge 1993), Ch.1 and p.50.
2   *The Future of Higher Education* (White Paper, Cm5735, Stationery Office 2003), ¶1.18.
3   Report of the National Committee of Inquiry into Higher Education (Chairman: Sir Ron Dearing), *Higher Education in the Learning Society* (NCIHE 1997), ¶8.17.

Which style to choose?

1   APA = American Psychological Association; ASA/ASR = American Sociological Association/American Sociological Review; CBE = Council of Biology Editors; AIP = American Institute of Physics.
2   R.M. Ritter, *The Oxford Guide to Style* (Oxford University Press 2002), p.505.
3   Primarily British Standards Institution, *BS 5605:1990 Recommendations for citing and referencing published material* (BSI 1990), but see also British Standards Institution, *BS 1629:1989 Recommendation for references to published materials.* (BSI 1989). (*BS 1629:1989* has been amended by BSI publication AMD 10180 published 15 November 1998, and *BS 5605:1990* has been amended by AMD 10182 published 15 December 1998.)

The conscientious student's predicament

1   'Last week a poll of 31 British universities by BBC Radio 4's *The World At One* "uncovered" what most academics already knew – that plagiarism has become a widespread practice. The survey found 1600 cases of plagiarism this year and most of the universities polled indicated that there has been a significant increase in cheating.' F. Furedi, 'Shortcut to success', *The Times Higher Education Supplement* (aka *The Times Higher*), 25 July, 2003.
2   See Peter J. Larkham, *Exploring and Dealing with Plagiarism: Traditional Approaches* http://online.northumbria.ac.uk/faculties/art/information_studies/Imri/JISCPAS/site/pubs_goodprac_larkham.asp. Accessed 9 August 2003. Also Hugh S. Pyper, *Avoiding Plagiarism, Advice for Students* http://online.northumbria.ac.uk/faculties/art/information_studies/Imri/JISCPAS/site/pubs_student_avoiding.asp. Accessed 8 October 2003.
3   University of London Regulations for the Degrees of MPhil and PhD, on the Birkbeck College website at http://www.bbk.ac.uk/reg/regulations/pdf/PhDregs.pdf. Accessed 30 April 2004.

How academic learning forces you to plagiarize

1 Diana Laurillard, *Rethinking University Education* (Routledge 1993), Ch.1 and p.50.
2 Jude Carroll and Jon Appleton (2001) *Plagiarism: A Good Practice Guide* http://www.jisc.ac.uk/pub01/brookes.pdf, p.8. Accessed 9 October 2003. Carroll and Appleton do acknowledge 'the irony and possible conflict of this situation in a report on the citation of others' ideas'.

Books on speed reading

All of these books are published in paperback and were in print in early 2004.

Colin Rose, *Accelerated Learning* (Accelerated Learning Systems 1985)
Paul R. Scheele, *Photoreading Whole Mind System* (3rd edition, Learning Strategies Corporation 1999)
Gordon Wainwright, *Read Faster, Recall More* (How To Books 2001)
Tony Buzan, *The Speed Reading Book* (Revised edition, BBC Worldwide 2003)
Tina Konstant, *Teach Yourself Speed Reading* (Hodder Headline 2003)

Acknowledgments

Many people have contributed, in many different ways, to the birth of this book. I owe a personal thank you to the following people:

The many students who over the years have talked to me about their experiences in higher education: it has been my privilege to work with them.

Paul Hobbs and Kathryn Redway, from whose courses on reading I have benefited.

Shona Mullen and her colleagues at the Open University Press, whose understanding, skill, dedication and drive I have every reason to appreciate.

Kate Pool and her colleagues of the Society of Authors, for practical and moral support.

John Levin for his informed comments on early drafts of this book, for the benefit of lessons he learned in the UK higher education system, for his invaluable help with IT and support in the ongoing battle with Dell and Microsoft products, and especially for the pleasure of his company.

Rachel Adriano, who recently re-entered the education system after a very long interval, and whose support for this project I value enormously.

Alice Pizer, for her belief in the importance of my work and writing.

Audrey Cleave, for demonstrating how a youthful, open mind can last and last.

Kevin Fitzgerald and Joe Geraghty, who both know about reinventing themselves: inspirations both.

Clare, Amy and Anne for their affection and encouragement and for road-testing some of the ideas in this book.

Gill, my wife, for her loving care and support, for the memorable times we have together, and for her tolerance (mostly) of a quirky, untidy and often preoccupied author.

Student-Friendly Guides

Sail through exams!

Preparing for traditional exams for undergraduates and taught postgraduates

A must for all students preparing for traditional exams!

This lively, short and to-the-point guide helps students prepare for exams in which they have two to three hours to answer a number of questions which they have not previously seen.

Written in a straightforward and supportive style, this guide:
– Enables students to take control of learning and revision
– Cuts through academic obfuscation
– Explains the language of exam questions

It provides a range of techniques and approaches which students can tailor to their own personal circumstances.

Practical, down to earth and on the side of the student, this invaluable resource helps all students to achieve their very best in exams.

Contents: The strange world of the university. READ THIS FIRST! – Introduction – Part One: Using past exam papers – Get hold of past exam papers – What to look for in past exam papers – Unfair questions – The guessing game: What topics will come up this year? – Part Two: Formulating model answers – What are examiners looking for? – Interpreting the question – Methodology – Materials – Drawing up a plan – An alternative approach: the 'question string' – Choose your introduction – Argument or chain of reasoning? – Writing exam answers: some more suggestions – Questions for examiners – Part Three: In the run-up to exam – Revising effectively – Memorizing – Make best use of your time – Getting in the right frame of mind for exams – Part Four: On the day of the exam – Be organized

112pp   0 335 21576 9   (Paperback)

Student-Friendly Guides

Successful teamwork!

For undergraduate and taught postgraduate students

This short, practical guide is for students who find themselves placed in groups and assigned a project to carry out.

– Allocating work appropriately
– Dealing with people who are taking a 'free-ride'
– Resolving disagreements
– Working constructively with people who they don't like very much.

The guide helps students to appreciate the tensions between the demands of the task, the needs of the team and individual's needs, and to understand why people behave as they do in a team situation. It provides reassurance when things get stressful, and helps students learn from the experience and make a success of their project.

Contents: Part One: Basics and Context – What do we mean by 'a team'? – The benefits of working in a team – Teamwork skills – Academic teamwork and the job market – Part Two: Getting Started – Get in your groups – Get to know one another – Formulate your ground rules – Check out your assignment and plan your work – Part Three: How are we Doing? – Progress on the project – Progress from 'group' to 'team' – Personal progress – Part Four: Perspectives on Team Behaviour – Tensions: the task, the team and the individual – Team roles – Management systems and team organization – Team development: forming, storming, norming, performing ... – The decision-making process – Negotiation – Cultural traits and differences – Individual traits: 'cats' and 'dogs' – Part Five: Teamwork Issues and Solutions – The task: getting the work done – Personal and inter-personal issues – Part Six: Benefiting from the Experience – Getting feedback – Reflection – Applying for jobs

112pp   0 335 21578 5 (Paperback)

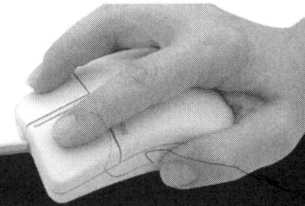